Publishing

IN THE DIGITAL AGE

GARETH WARD

Sponsored by

BOWERDEAN
Publishing Company Limited

Work in the Digital Age

A new series of books explaining how the 'new technology' – the Internet, CD-ROM, on-line services, virtual reality etc. – will have an impact on work of different kinds. Titles already published include *Financial Services in the Digital Age* by Paul Gosling, *Retail in the Digital Age* by Nigel Cope, *Travel in the Digital Age* by Linsey McNeil and *Government in the Digital Age* by Paul Gosling. *Education in the Digital Age* by Dorothy Walker is published in May 1998.

Published by The Bowerdean Publishing Company Ltd.
of 8 Abbotstone Road, London SW15 1QR

First published in 1998

Gareth Ward has asserted his right under the Copyright, Designs and Patents Act, 1988, to be identified as Author of this Work.

British Library Cataloguing-in-Publication Data.
A catalogue record for this book is available from the British Library.

ISBN 0 906097 94 0

Designed by the Senate
Printed by Interprint Ltd., Malta

CONTENTS

GLOSSARY

Acrobat: the program for creating pdf files. It allows for the editing of those files.

Bandwith: the size of the pipe that allows the flow of digital information.

Browser: the software that allows you to look at a Web page. Examples are Internet Explorer from Microsoft and Navigator from Netscape.

Digital Printing: printing without a plate or other master image. It may be inkjet or a technology that has a laser write a latent image on a specially coated drum which then attracts toner particles or ink. These are transferred to paper and may be fixed by heat. The image can be rewritten for each turn of the drum.

Document Type Definition (DTD): the table of values for body type and headlines that is at the head of an SGML document. The recipient of the file can replace the standard codes with different typefaces to alter the appearance of the document.

File Transfer Protocol (FTP): the protocol for moving files across the Internet. FTP site is an address to which files are transferred before being called into a new network.

Hyper Text Mark up Language (HTML): the language of the Web browser. Standard instructions that obey HTML rules dictate the appearance of the Web pages though the appearance will be different depending on factors such as how large the viewing area is.

Integrated Services Digital Network (ISDN): a high bandwith telecommunications cable for linking two points that has greater capacity than voice-only lines. A single ISDN line nominally has a bandwith of 64Kb/sec. Several ISDN lines can operate in parallel.

Java: the first platform independent operating language. A programming language that works within the browser and regardless of the type of computer the operator has. The program produced in Java is called an applet.

Local Area Network: the linking of several computers or peripheral devices by cable in a single office or building.

Page Description Language: a computer program that describes the position of every element on a printed page.

Portable Document Format (pdf): a format developed by Adobe for displaying pages on a screen with the integrity of appearance of a printed paper page. A document in pdf can be printed as well as viewed in a Web browser. The pdf is generated with Adobe Acrobat or a number of other applications.

PostScript: the building block of the desktop publishing revolution. A page description language that is resolution independent. Pages created in a desktop program will always have the same visual appearance within the limitations of the printing device. PostScript is supported by thousands of software programs and as many printers, including digital presses.

Print on Demand: the method of printing just the required number of copies as and where they are required. Involves digital printing and organisation of databases.

Raster Image Processor: the Rip interprets the page description language and drives the output device. Lasers image in lines across a page, building up the image in successive sweeps of the raster head. Most Rips are PostScript or pdf Rips, designed to work with PostScript or pdf pages.

Standard Generalised Mark up Language (SGML): a set of agreed codes to define headings, footnotes and other niceties that make up the appearance of a page. The SGML code defines what those elements are. It does not dictate the typeface or sizes that are to be used.

Universe Resource Locator: the address of a Web page or other Internet Resource.

Wide Area Network: a network that links Local Area Networks together, usually using public networks such as the telephone system.

World Wide Web: the part of the Internet that includes support for graphics, moving images and sound. It was with the announcement of the WWW that the Internet left the realm of the specialist and academic and became important for wider use.

Extensible Mark up Language (XML): a simplified version of SGML and an improvement on HTML, allowing the creation of more sophisticated Web page designs, including overlapping text and images.

Extensible Style Language (XSL): the framework for the XML document and a style sheet template for XML.

❶ 2010

The alarm rang as usual at 7.30, waking first Alan Leyland then the whole of the Leyland family. As Alan lurched out of bed to head for the bathroom, sensors picked up his steps to turn the kettle on, ready for that essential first cup of tea. Downstairs the inkjet printer also woke up, spewing out the three pages of the so called Daily Leyland. The Daily Leyland was a newspaper made up of news and features of special interest to the Leyland family. The contents came from items culled daily from the Internet, in accordance with a range of interest areas specified by each member of the family. John, the 23 year old who, much to his mother's disgust, still lived at home, had given this name to the family on-line newspaper five years ago and it had stuck. While his father was in the bathroom he dashed downstairs to grab the three pages. It had been six pages until they had bought the duplex colour inkjet printer last year which had enabled him to print on both sides at once. The first page provided the news the family had said it was interested in. This had often led to lively discussions around the dinner table. The paper consisted of items culled automatically from the Internet on subjects which the family had specified. They had been asked to fill in a palette of preferences and had been able to choose what kind of stories they would like to read. They had gone for an eclectic range which included novelists, aerospace, cookery, Liverpool FC, any particular share prices and pop groups. John had recently added Argentina to the list since he was planning a trip to the booming South American country later in the year. His sister Jennifer, still at university, had requested a syndicated cartoon strip that wasn't otherwise available in the UK.

Cicely Leyland considered herself up to date with technology and was certainly more prepared to exploit its potential than many of her friends, but still preferred the conventional newspapers and magazines delivered with the groceries each morning. The writing in the Daily Leyland was too flat, too matter of fact, she complained and of course there was almost no advertising. She liked advertising. It kept her up to date with new products and sparked her imagination. How else would she know what that bright red car was if she hadn't seen the ads? Her husband pointed out to her that she should subscribe to magazines like he did. That meant filling in a detailed personal profile of her likes and dislikes, her interests and ambitions as well as paying the subscription for the magazine. That way, the publisher could tailor the ads the magazine carried to match her interests, perhaps even having ads that were addressed to her personally. Some publishers offered reduced rates for information of value that they in turn could use to pull in advertisers. "Too much like junk mail," she insisted.

Today she planned to pick up the new Delia Smith cookbook from the local bookshop. She had printed out the first chapter from the publisher's Web site the night before on the inkjet printer, enjoyed it and had ordered the full copy from the publisher there and then. The bookshop, if it could be called a bookshop, would have the book printed and bound ready for collection at 11am. Once her order had been received, the text and images had been downloaded from the publisher's database and transmitted to the digital press in the bookshop's backroom. It would print the entire 386 page (pp) volume, which would emerge collated and adhesive bound, ready for insertion into the case binding.

While at the bookshop, which was a member of a chain owned by a printer, she would probably pick up a paperback or two. Agatha Christie and Catherine Cookson remained thankfully immune to the march of digital technology. These were still available as recognisable paperback books bought from the bookshop, supermarket or railway station in the traditional way. What she could not see was the vast changes that had taken place in the production of the paperback. Publishers and printers were even beginning to experiment with paper produced in factories from artificially created cellulose rather than from trees or other plant life.

John Leyland had recently started a new job selling legal and financial advice.

One advantage of the job was that he rarely had to call in to the office. He was what, ten years before, would have been called a virtual salesman. He no longer had great piles of literature describing the various products his company sold, nor did he need the huge tomes on the intricacies of financial law that used to line many an office. Instead the same information came on CD-ROM with a user-friendly search engine added. If he needed to access a piece of arcane case law he could find it in seconds. The relevant page of the book – for everybody still thought of the silver plastic disc as a book – would be called to the screen and could be printed from the back of the portable computer he used as an essential tool of his trade.

He needed to update the information periodically and rather than replace one disk with another, John plugged the computer into the Internet port and downloaded the data direct from head office. As he worked he would be unaware whether the page on screen was one that had come from the CD, from the computer's hard disk or perhaps, if he was still connected to head office, from the company's data base. On each occasion the page would be identical in appearance.

After work, John planned to use the same computer and CD-ROM to help restore the 50 year old Singer car he had in pieces across the garage. It was no longer worth anybody's while printing manuals for such a vehicle, but the CD was available by mail order and had advantages over the paper-based version. He could view that carburettor from all angles – see it in far greater detail than on the black and white image and some versions had video clips to show how to carry out the intricate adjustments.

His sister of course loathed the car mechanics. She was studying at university, though it seemed that she was rarely on the campus. She constantly explained that apart from the social life, the occasional lecture and her tutorials, there was little need to enter the buildings. She had an E-book, a folder sized computer screen that had radio and ir (infra red) transmitter and receiver connections. This she checked for the latest reading list and browsed through the academic articles needed for the next essay. She could annotate those pieces as if with a marker pen on a piece of paper, something her father swore he had never done in his student days. Once written, of course, the essay would be sent direct to her tutor's e-mail queue.

The E-book was light enough to be carried anywhere and robust enough to be used inside or out. As a computer it was not powerful enough to run anything but rudimentary applications such as wordprocessing and e-mail. However the real computer was on her desk. That contained her course work so far and, should she come to a write a PhD thesis, that too would be composed on the computer. Her assessor would also read it in digital form and it would be published digitally also – though its readership would be very small.

Certainly her father, who was a cottage publisher, would not look at her thesis. He was plagued by unsolicited manuscripts arriving by e-mail and sure enough that morning there were two more in his basket when he reached his office.

The office was one of a number in a converted farm. Barns, a cattle shed and outbuildings had been converted to provide a number of small businesses with office accommodation. These were people who previously would have had to have had offices in the city but thanks to strong digital communications links, could operate from more congenial surroundings. As well as the conventional computer, Alan Leyland had a wall-mounted flat screen used for video conferencing and a flat desktop computer that, unlike the Apple Mac or IBM PC, was a true desktop computer in that it unrolled to take the place of the desk top. Simple icons could call up the in-tray, work in progress and work completed. Like his daughter's E-book, the desktop computer had a touch-sensitive screen to allow digital annotation of the electronic paper in front of him. A touch in the corner of the sheet would turn that one over and bring up the next in sequence.

The computer with the box-like monitor was a powerful NC machine. Switched on it brought up the familiar Netscape opening screen. Netscape had become the bête noir of computers, usurping the role played by Microsoft a dozen years earlier. Bill Gates had left the software business to concentrate on his digital assets. He had used the billions built up through Microsoft to acquire digital rights to every painting he could. Gates was the digital master of a greater collection of artworks than any collector in history – certainly greater than any national collection.

Alan Leyland would have to grapple with the Gates Foundation later in the day when selecting images to accompany the new travel guide he was working on. First would come some basic editing and copywriting. The program was called to the Super NC from the database maintained by the service provider that he paid fees to. This had the latest versions of all standard programs. It was reassuring to know that there was no longer any need to keep checking that he was using the latest version of all software.

The travel guides he was working on would appear simultaneously in electronic and paper format. And he would maintain the database to allow readers to check that the information they wanted was as up to date as possible. The almost instant obsolescence of travel guides was a problem that Leyland hoped to overcome with this project. The book would be available as a conventional publication from a range of outlets. He'd negotiated a deal to allow travel operators to print extracts to provide for their customers in their holiday documentation.

The book would also be available on its own dedicated Web site, giving the publisher the opportunity to carry frequently updated material. This might include a new restaurant review, changes in opening times of museums and galleries or alterations to bus routes and train timetables – all the facts that were liable to change between commissioning and publication of a book in the old days. A subscription to the Web site, offered initially with the book and updated annually, would mean never having to buy a more up to date edition of the paper product. The CD version of the book would also include video clips to illustrate the text. The traveller could visit the city of her choice before getting there.

The raw text Leyland received needed to be edited so that its integrity remained, whatever format was chosen for publication, paper or digital. The images to accompany the text would be pulled from digital libraries like those established by many photographic agencies towards the end of the 20th century, or from the electronic collections built by the likes of Bill Gates. Electronic fingerprinting with invisible watermarks ensured that no unofficial reproduction was possible.

Collected text and images would be sent electronically to the designer, and from there to the printer or to the Web site, with no need for paper. Proofs would be sent back electronically to the quality colour printer sitting in Leyland's office. Should something more be required, across in another building was the high volume colour

Xerox machine shared between all the businesses on the site. He could use this later in the day to run off a dozen copies of the first guide to hand to the sales agents who would need a printed copy to show the buyers from major book chains.

▲   ▲   ▲

A L L these innovations are within our grasp. Certain areas of the publishing world are nearer the digital dream than others. Academic publishers are already prepared to forego print and provide pure electronic information. Printing presses exist that can take digital input and produce just one book at a time. The colour that the digital press can reproduce is improving in quality all the time and the cost of using and owning such equipment is dropping. Technologies such as CD-ROM, the Internet and the World Wide Web are starting to change the paradigm for publishers. The options are increasing. But it is already apparent that there will not be an immediate switch from conventional publishing to electronic, and indeed that not all publications will be suited to electronic production.

The easiest distinction is between 'need to know' and 'nice to know'. As a rule of thumb, the more up to date and essential the information, the more likely it is to be published electronically. This does not mean that readers will not use paper. It is likely, especially for long documents, that users will print out the document but using their own printer. Up to the minute legal, financial, business-to-business communications will move to electronic forms. So too will those publications that have only a limited readership – academic journals being a prime example. The size of the market is so small that conventional printing technology is no longer feasible.

At the other end of the spectrum will be the coffee table art books where quality of reproduction is everything. Lithographic printing on paper has reached the point of near perfection when using the latest techniques and machinery. The cost will come down and much smaller print runs will become economic, but litho printing will remain for publications where the highest quality is needed. Litho printing will also retain its place for long runs needed in the shortest space of time – as in the case of newspapers.

Conventional print will remain for magazines also, but as publishers gather information on the readers of those magazines, by encouraging subscriptions, buying lists of credit card users, airline users etc., they will be able to offer more and more personalised publications. Already the editorial is configured in this way – otherwise why would there need to be several dozen women's magazines instead of just one? But the advertising remains general. This will change.

❷ Overview

FOR the first time in 500 years, the power of the printing press is under challenge. Respected names like Caxton, Gutenberg, Heidelberg and Linotype are giving way to the likes of Xerox, IBM, Adobe and Siemens. And the challenge to the printed book is increasing as never before. Publishers can no longer take their product for granted. Nevertheless it will take a cultural revolution as well as a technological revolution to remove the book from its place on the shelf.

▲   ▲   ▲

If dreams of the paperless office, have faded, nevertheless digital means of conveying information are going to become much more important. However it is not all bad news for paper. According to CAP Ventures, a respected US consultancy firm, US paper consumption will grow from 43.7m tons in 1995 to 65.6 million tons in 2015. Project leader Adina Levin comments: "The information explosion has led to increased consumption of paper, but we find that the linear growth of paper is slower than the exponential growth in the amount of information."

The value of electronic documents is growing by leaps and bounds. The world wide value of electronic document revenue in 1991, according to the Electronic Document Systems Foundation (EDSF) figures, stood at $46.9bn; by 1996 this had grown to $85.7bn and it is projected to reach

$152.3bn by 2001. The value is doubling every five years, putting the market at $600bn by 2010. These projections are conservative.

Much of what is printed now on conventional machinery will move to digital printing methods, particularly reference, educational and professional and scientific books. The revolution begun by Gutenberg, where it became possible to produce multiple copies of a book for the first time, is being overturned. In the near future the economics of book production, where the greater the number of units produced the lower the cost, will be turned upside down. It could be just as cheap to print a single copy, close to the point of need, as to print thousands of copies, store them in warehouses and ship them in small numbers to specialist shops. All parts of the publishing business will be changed by the digital revolution, which is giving the reader – the consumer – the power to decide where and how they want to read a publication. Book, magazine or newspaper publishers, as well as bookshops, will have to rise to meet the challenge. For the first time paper is no longer essential for the spread of information.

It will be perfectly possible to print a book at home, using desktop laser or inkjet printers, though this will be impractical for a number of reasons (see Chapter 4). It will also be possible to edit a book at home so that it combines chapters from several other books. The work is totally unique in that the combination of chapters and material may be unique to that user. The material will be offered by publishers on the understanding that the readers can select what is on offer and compile a collection of articles for their personal use alone – all thanks to digital technology.

This poses problems and creates opportunities for everyone involved in the publishing process – authors, publisher, printers, newsagents and booksellers. At the heart of the challenge is the Internet – quite simply the greatest development in publishing and information dissemination since Gutenberg introduced moveable type to Europe. Driving this is digital information, bits and bytes that have more power than the '26 soldiers of lead' associated with conventional printing. Digital information does not need paper nor lengthy preparation before printing. However the demands of the digital age do need to be understood. If information is not to be printed, how will it be published – on a standard computer screen, on a flat display, a roll up computer or in an electronic book? Whatever is published will almost certainly involve the Internet.

THE INTERNET AND INTRANETS

The Internet is an unimaginably vast network of individual computers hooked up to others that act as file servers to store huge amounts of data. It has been around for many years, but until the scientists working for the Cern laboratory in Switzerland developed what became the World Wide Web (the Web), it was limited in its use. The World Wide Web added the ability to display images and add sound and moving graphics and films to the Internet file. The file evolved into the Web page, the on-line equivalent of printed catalogues, brochures or other promotional items. Equally the Internet can hold academic journals, magazines and entire libraries of books. It is no coincidence that the basic window used to access this mountain of information is known as a Web page. Access is via a computer modem and a Web browser interface – a sort of digital taxi service that takes you from site to site. But at the moment it is a slow process. The standard transfer rate is 28.8 kps (kilobytes per second), which is uncomfortable except for the simplest of pages. By 2010 this frustration will seem odd, for data access rates will no longer impede the use of the Internet. A number of possible solutions are being developed, including the adaptation of existing infrastructures – using the electricity supply grid to supply data access – or creating new infrastructures such as a network of low orbit satellites. The ability to transfer data more quickly will vastly increase the richness of the Internet experience. Film and sound will spark entire channels of Web programming. Visual telephony will be commonplace.

A battle is currently being fought for the position of dominant Web browser supplier between Netscape and Microsoft. The differences between the two are slight, but well before 2010 a Web browser of one sort will be the standard interface on all computers. The sons of Quark, Excel etc. will be retrieved, not through a Mac interface or Windows 95 or Unix, each of which is slightly different. Once called up on these different operating systems the standard programs can work slightly differently. Quark on a PC is different to Quark on a Mac and requires some adjustment on the part of the user. The browser will act as as a standard layer between the computer and the application. Because the layer is standard as far as the application is concerned, all versions of the different applications will be the same to the user. There will also be a tremendous amount in common between different applications making file movements between one and the other straightforward. There will be no need to learn how to operate different computers, since all will be controlled through the same browser interface. The user, working through a browser, will neither know nor care whether the resources accessed are kept on the computer's hard disk, in some form of intermediate storage like a CD-ROM or floppy disk, a nearby file server or one on the other side of the globe. Operators will be able to move from one computer to another and still have access to information on their own computer.

For computer software developers the advantage will be that only one version of a software application will be needed, since by operating with the browser it will run on any computer platform. Object oriented programming, the digital equivalent of building with ready made bricks, will speed the development of new software, often meeting the specific needs of one customer.

While the Internet is a public network, private networks using the same technology – called intranets– are going to proliferate. They have the same advantages as the wider Internet, but because access is restricted to an organisation or corporation, it is only available to those the corporation wishes to include. Intranets will replace standard computer networks and will provide substantial benefits to IT departments. These will include freedom from dependence on one type of computer and from the necessity for all those using the company network to be located in a specific office. There will also be a saving in training.

Software could come from the Net, but is most likely to come from intranets. The different applications will be held in a central 'library' and the user can 'borrow' an application – Word, Excel or whatever – for a while, replacing it when the task is finished. Today the user has to buy all the applications. But once a dominant broswer has established itself, it will make no difference what kind or version of computer is being used, once the library has updated its version of the application, all the users on the intranet will also be updated immediately. The intranet provides this freedom.

Intranets will be extended to cover suppliers and customers who will be allowed access to certain areas of a company network. Interaction between external partners will be as easy as it is between departments in the same company. Files and jobs created in the production process will move instantly over any distance. The motorcycle courier is living on borrowed time.

FLAT SCREENS, ELECTRONIC INK AND CD-ROMS

However good and user-friendly screen-based displays are going to become – and they will become very good indeed – paper will remain. Screens are currently based on cathode ray tube (CRT) electron guns, a technology that has been refined since the days of John Logie Baird, but is intrinsically the same. Flat screens are coming. A Xerox spin-off has announced a high quality, high resolution colour monitor, suitable for graphic arts professionals and developments of this will percolate down to lower levels of the market. The conventional screen will be considered an anachronism within a decade.

Other flat screen technologies are developments of those used in portable lap top computers and more interestingly those developed for military use, where flat head-up displays are used in aircraft and tanks. Screens will appear as wall hangings or may be built into desks flush with the work surface. The computer itself will be controlled via a graphics tablet, touch-sensitive screen or voice command. The barrier between screen and paper will fade, with no clear edge between where one ends and the other begins. Flat screen technologies will have none of the size limitations that afflict CRT screens and will consume far less power.

Developments such as Electronic Ink, which has emerged from the Massachusetts Institute of Technology, and is now the subject of a venture capital backed start up called E Ink Corporation, will blur the boundary even more. The electronic ink technology is based on a microencapsulated micromechanical display – in other words a piece of flexible plastic or paper material that requires far less power than any computer display, and which it will be possible to bind into book form. The nearest current equivalent is the scoreboard at Lords Cricket Ground, where hundreds of small discs are painted white on one side, black on the other. In response to computer control, these show one side or the other, either creating figures or not. The E Ink project is emulating this approach at a micro engineering level. Should this line of development succeed, electronic paper will prove to be the Holy Grail sought since Xerox scientists at Palo Alto in California came up with the electronic book concept in the late 1970s.

Several types of electronic book are close to reaching the market now and will be improved in subsequent years. Others are currently drawings in offices or ideas lodged in an engineer's mind. Issues such as weight and restricted battery life will be addressed, but the big question is whether the product will have only a very short life before being overtaken by other technologies.

The medium that has come to be associated with electronic and multipublication beyond all others is the CD-ROM. The small silver platter is already accepted as preferable to the reference book. With the advent of digital versatile disks (DVDs), with ten times the storage capacity of the CD-ROM, the next generation of silver platters will open further opportunities, taking the reference book beyond words into sound and movement. Sales of multi-media CDs are climbing, even before DVDs come on the scene. Wrangles over the precise standards for the new medium are dogging its birth, particularly in respect of specifications for the rewritable digital disk.

Yet this may become a non-starter in the face of the Internet. The Internet and the networks it will help establish are already being used to sell and promote books and magazines and it is taking over some of the classified advertising that has been the traditional province of newspapers.

The Internet is without doubt the most powerful communications medium the world has yet known, with the same revolutionary power that the first printing presses had. The individual can, with luck or skill, locate and retrieve information from across the globe. The databases that hold what is now disparate information, are going to become better organised and structured to improve the chances of finding what is required. Publishers, used to the dynamics of paper based information, are going to have to become equally adept at running databases. Many are already doing so, but in specialist areas only. Intranets are going to change the way publishers work.

DIGITAL TECHNOLOGY AND PRINTING

The means that will bring all this about is digital technology in every sense. Pages that at one time were set in lead, so that second and subsequent impressions were exactly that – impressions from the same pages of set type – are giving way to digital matter that can be reconfigured to suit any purpose. Standing lead type has long ago given way to photographic film and aluminium litho plates, but the principle that origination is difficult means that standing film and plates will still be used for reprints.

Refinements of this system and the dominance of the offset litho process since the 1970s and its improvement in the years since, has made modern book production close to an industrial scale process and reduced unit manufacturing costs year by year. New production techniques will close the gap between digital prepress and the mechanical printing process. Press control systems mean it is possible to predict with accuracy how long a job will take, and litho presses are reaching speeds unheard of five years ago.

It is no surprise that offset litho printing is the dominant printing process. It is a far more flexible process in terms of colour reproduction than letterpress, which cannot match litho's quality, or gravure, which cannot match its cost effectiveness. Litho can handle the simplest pamphlet and the finest quality facsimile printing. The printing press at the end of the 20th century can be operated from a console set apart from the machine. The plates can be removed and mounted automatically, servo motors move plates and cylinders into line thus achieving perfect register, while others calculate settings for feeder, grippers, pressure and ink ducts. With eight printing units on a sheetfed press, full colour pages can be printed on both sides of the sheet simultaneously.

There is minimal start up waste and within an hour several thousands sheets can be ready for folding. Web offset printing cannot yet match sheetfed printing for its start up speed and flexibility, but it produces folded sections from the press, which has time and cost benefits when binding. It is therefore the chosen printing method for longer print runs, for newspapers and magazines, where speed from publisher to reader is the important factor. For book work, web offset printing has restrictions in terms of the paper that can be used.

The efficiency of modern printing technology has encouraged the take up of Just in Time production, following the example of the Japanese. The customer orders fewer numbers in the first instance, but frequent reprints of small deliveries as sales climb. If sales do not warrant reprints, the publishers have reduced their exposure. There are no piles of unsold books clogging up expensive warehouses and bookshops, waiting to be remaindered or pulped.

The seeds that will end the supremacy of the offset process were sown 50 years ago. The first electrophotographic copier – the Xerox machine – appeared. No skills were needed to reproduce multiple copies of any sheet of paper. But the technology was of little use to the printing industry until, in 1991, Xerox introduced the Docutech, the first digital printing press (though not recognised as such at the time). The digital press differs from a copier in that there is no original in a printed form to be copied. Instead the original is a digital page, which is transformed into a series of electronic signals to drive the laser. Instead of an optical system to convey the image to the printer drum, a laser is used to write the image of the page to the drum. This in turn attracts particles of toner which can be transferred to the paper. A heating element fuses the toner to the paper.

There are limitations to the process in terms of the types of paper that can be used and the resolution of the image. At the outset, 300 dots per inch (dpi) was the maximum quality obtainable. This was soon raised to 600dpi, which has been considered acceptable in most type sizes. The limitations on moving to finer resolutions have been the toner particle size, the resolving power of the lasers and the speed at which data could be transferred to the laser. All these obstacles will be temporary. Data transfer rates will increase as a result of computer industry developments. When Gigabit transmission becomes viable, data transmission speed ceases to be an issue.

The arrival of blue diode lasers promises to end the limitations of image resolution. These lasers, invented in the mid 1990s, will quickly become commercial devices applicable to a number of purposes. The main impetus is addressing data on a CD, increasing the capacity of the disk. This is a massive market and gives developers the incentive to pour millions into research. The imaging and printing industry benefits as a side effect.

Developing finer toner particles is a matter of preventing them sticking together. An ultra thin wax coating is one way of doing this. In any case toner particle size is not going to prevent the quality of electrophotostatic print engines being improved.

Another approach is to do away with toner powder and instead use a liquid toner. This is a technique developed by Benny Landa and applied first in the short-lived Electropress and with greater success in the Indigo digital colour press. There were four versions of the Electropress, one of which was intended to print books. This was a co-development between AM International, the press's developer, RR Donnelley as the printer and McGraw Hill the publisher. However the project foundered (see Chapter 5).

That idea was ahead of its time and the technology to make it a success. The reasons it failed to catch on were as much cultural as technical. It seems that lecturers at US colleges were unable to decide at the beginning of the semester what papers they would be using in their courses. The issue of copyright did not arise, since this was held by McGraw Hill. However the very exclusivity of the deal also acted against its chances of success. Other publishers, other printers, other press developers were excluded, but the genie was out of the bottle. McGraw Hill continues to work on the custom book concept with a true print-on-demand application that will shortly use laser printers located close to the point of use.

POSTSCRIPT

The most important enabling technology propelling the development of digital publishing was the development of PostScript as a device independent, page description language. The same page, document or book could be output on any compatible printer, at whatever resolution, with no effect on the appearance of the page itself. The publishing industry was freed from the tyranny of working within a type library from a foundry like Linotype or Monotype and having to use that company's typesetting systems.

PostScript evolved into Level 2 PostScript, adding features for colour printing, and now into PostScript 3, which Adobe has optimised for publishing on the Web. PostScript is a programming language which provides developers with a great deal of functionality. But it has the undesirable side effect that developers can inadvertently create applications producing slightly different versions of PostScript which can mean the same file being produced in a slightly different way by different imagesetters. The inconsistency is overcome with Adobe Acrobat, which works with a format that Adobe calls the portable document format (pdf).

There are several key advantages to publishers with this format. First it is a more compact format, with just the layers needed to reproduce the page. The impact on file sizes can be substantial, with important implications for transmitting pages digitally. Secondly, it is a document independent format. To access a PostScript page within a long document can take time, because the interpreter needs to go to the top of the file to discover what fonts are needed. This is not necessary in pdf, since typographic information is held in each page, allowing a user to go direct to the page in question. Thirdly, pdf is a true 'what you see is what you get' format. There are no different ways of reading a pdf page. Once the page is correct and in the pdf format, the publisher can be confident that anyone looking at that page on any computer screen anywhere in the world, will be looking at identical pages.

This makes pdf perfect for document management purposes, where the aim is to reuse information in the same, or visually identical format. This is ideal when spin-off publications are contemplated, either as part of the main publication or for distribution in other territories. Customers can call pdf pages from a database and use them to suit their own purposes. Security features can be added, for example a watermark that appears when printed. Future refinements are going to address an inability to handle colour to the degree that the printing industry requires. It will also offer integration of sound and moving images.

Brook House is an Oxfordshire company that is already working extensively with pdf. It has created a pdf version of the Royal Pharmaceutical Society's *British National Formulary*, a 700,000 circulation guide to prescribing drugs. This is now published on CD-ROM and was designed to replicate the look and feel of the printed version as much as possible. Its managing director Roy Walter is enthusiastic about pdfs. "They look exactly like the original document, are not platform reliant, are fully searchable and offer limitless republishing opportunities across networks, the Internet, CD -ROM or even on paper."

The biggest drawback is that once a page is in the pdf format, it is as good as locked. There is only limited opportunity to edit the file and no chance to reformat the content for use on a different medium. For publishers wanting this freedom, the standardised general mark up language (SGML) is what is required. This allows the same text to be reformatted automatically according to publisher decided rules and to suit different purposes. The World Wide Web hypertext mark up language, which has to display the same Web page on a number of browsers, is a close relation to SGML.

At some point in the next few years, hypertext mark up language (HTML) is going to become part of the pdf structure, while Web centred documents are going to become richer thanks to sound and motion. This will demand a different format to HTML which is limited in the design sense. The candidates for this are XML, the eXtensible mark up language and XSL, the eXtensible style language. Both these will

---

SGML, standardised general mark up language, is a way of assigning values or styles to elements on a page that remain constant. This can include the headline, introduction, any footnotes, various paragraph styles and body text for example. A DTD – document type definition – acts as a translation table and puts real typographic values against the marked up elements. By using a different DTD, with different widths or typefaces, the look of a document can be changed, but the placement of the elements remains constant relative to the other elements. This is used when moving from one sized page to another and now in moving from a paper document to an electronic presentation. It is not always desirable to replicate the appearance of a portrait page on a screen which does not share the same dimensional aspect.

If however it is important to retain the shape and appearance of the paper document, then the Adobe portable document format (pdf) is the choice. Once the page has been converted into the pdf format it is effectively locked and its appearance cannot easily be changed. The page will look exactly the same in one medium as in another and will use the best resolution to do so.

For printing companies, pdf will be the preferred format since the page received from the publisher will always have the appearance passed for press by the customer. The printer cannot be blamed for any errors since he cannot be responsible for altering the file. SGML on the other hand may be preferred by the publisher, who may want to reconfigure the data in a different medium or a different book. A copy of Alice in Wonderland in pdf will always look the same, whereas an SGML version can have different typefaces and headline styles merely by altering the DTD.

---

overcome the problems of building electronic commerce applications. XML will allow individual user interfaces to be generated according to the style preferred by the user.

John Tigue, a software designer with DataChannel, a leading

supporter of XML, told a conference, "What if you had an XML DTD (document type definition) that described directories? The user could log on and have his entire user interface generated based on a DTD and presented on the fly [without delay]. And the data could be anywhere." The XSL version is being supported by Microsoft, unlike XML, which is a committee supported standard. Developers are already beginning to lean towards XSL.

These formats also fit in with formats like Java, or ActiveX, which are the first building blocks towards operating system independent computing. Java works through a Web browser and downloads small pieces of program called Applets, as and when needed. There is no reason why a publishing system should not be built around Java, with the individual reporters and editors calling down the Applets they need when required. A distributed system like this could replace the massive networks of dedicated terminals used by all newspaper and magazine publishers today.

In terms of hard copy printing, electrostatic and laser printing are themselves being challenged. Xerox has recently bought the entire share capital of Canadian company Delphax, which specialises in printing machines using magnetography. Instead of using lasers to create the latent image on the drum by changing their electrostatic charge, the particles on the magnetography drum have their magnetic polarity altered. It is used today on high speed printers.

A further technology widely used, from the high speed specialist printer to desktop units, is inkjet printing. In reality the term covers a range of technologies using different types of inks suiting different requirements. Its simplicity and relatively low cost makes inkjet an ideal technology for widespread use. The current drawbacks lie with the intricacies of manufacturing printing heads and the low speed of production. However British company Xaar, owner of a fistful of patents around piezo head inkjets, (piezo is a small piece of crystal that can be made to vibrate by the application of an electrical current) is convinced that 120pp a minute inkjet printing, in full colour, is not only possible but also not far away. Xaar has been achieving resolutions of 720dpi. Within the next ten years other forms of digital printing, including offset litho variants using re-imageable cylinders, will come to the market. Their success or otherwise will be dictated by cost and reliability and by how much of the market has been conceded to electrophotographic and ink jet printers.

Conventional printing technologies have already adapted to digital technology. It is impossible to operate a modern printing machine without digital controls, and these will become progressively more sophisticated as presses which can accept some kind of digital imaging are developed. Even without digital printing the modern offset printing press is going to be far more productive and efficient than its predecessors. Colour printing will be of a far higher quality, set up times much shorter and printing speeds higher. Automated equipment in the bindery will cut turnaround times from weeks to days.

Other systems of digital printing are going to emerge and will take the resolution beyond 720dpi and speed beyond 1,000ppm. Japanese developers are already discussing the concept of a 1,200dpi laser. This would require the development of suitable toners and the network speeds to receive and process much larger volumes of data. Nothing is insurmountable in technology terms. Publishers will get to grips with the digital age. They must, for there is no guarantee that the industry leaders of today will maintain their position in the digital age.

❸ Publishers

T H E digital revolution will force massive changes to the way publishers operate. Those that do not change will become increasingly uncompetitive and will ultimately go out of business if they haven't already been snapped up by a more successful predator.

▲   ▲   ▲

Apart from specialist publishers – professional, business, educational etc. – where unit sales and costs are reasonably predictable, book publishing, with its large overheads, high failure rate and dependence on skilled people, has not always sat well within the modern corporation with shareholders to satisfy. Reed-Elsevier enjoys publishing academic and legal texts, but has been keen to sell Reed Consumer Books; Viacom a huge entertainment conglomerate has been equally keen to sell Simon & Schuster. Book publishing comes with 500 years of tradition and established working practices. Unfortunately it can provide relatively few guaranteed best-selling authors, compared to the 100,000 new titles published in the UK alone each year. The structure looks as if it will become too unwieldy for the digital age. Book publishing needs to change.

In the UK, the Net Book Agreement for many years acted as a comfort blanket. Books were different and did not need to compete in the same aggressive way as other consumer durables. The Net Book Agreement is no more. By 2010 books will not have gone away, but the means of creating them will have undergone substantial changes.

The current system sees an author working with a more or less simple word-processing program. Publishers still like to see hard copy, so although a disk may be the means of delivery, the contents are going to be printed out and worked on by hand. There may be no contact between publisher and author during the creative process. This is short-sighted, especially as authors will inevitably deliver their work late. The new way of working will bring the author into the publisher's network. E-mail already serves as a way of communicating, but it is crude in comparison with the much richer electronic mail systems that are pushing their way into the market as a result of working through Internet browsers.

The author will be working on a computer linked via the Internet to the publisher. With improved data transfer rates, distance will not be a problem and the wide area network will be as fast as the local area network for moving electronic information. A local area network is one confined to a single office or building. A wide area network involves many buildings across larger distances. It may be based on telephone cable, an intranet or the Internet. The software will emulate the way of working as now, with editor and author being able to make changes to a document simultaneously, although that document will not be physically present for either.

This can happen in a crude way now. Adobe's Acrobat software, which uses its pdf file structure, is designed to display documents electronically with the same integrity as a paper document. The page on screen looks exactly the same as the printed page on the desk. With the Acrobat pdf reader, almost the most popular program in the world, it is possible to read the pdf files on any computer and perhaps to print them off. With the Acrobat software itself, editing the pdf file becomes possible, either by adding the digital equivalent of Post-It notes to points in the text, or by rewriting the text. Future versions of this software will allow the editing process to go on simultaneously on the same document but from different computers. With video telephony, another technology that will be in place by 2010, the author need never leave his or her garret and the publisher need never venture out to lunch.

The design stage of book production will increasingly work like the writing, with freelance designers operating from studios which are linked, when necessary, to the publisher's network. That network will store all the relevant details of a book in the production process, allowing intimate monitoring of each stage of production. In addition, information from sales and marketing teams, in-house or bought in specially, will be fed to the network and added to the project's files. If initial sales predictions change, up or down, the system will automatically adjust as necessary. This may be as crude as altering the print run; or it could mean the network deciding to change the format of the book, if permitted to do so; or switching automatically to a different printer if the numbers are now not within that printer's optimum capacity. Production orders will be raised or cancelled and communicated to the production system at the print supplier. There will be no wasted calls or meetings.

The sales function will also change as a result of the digital network. Marketing and promotion now mainly consist in selling the title to the booksellers via representatives on the ground, or ads in the trade press, and to the public via consumer advertising on posters, in the press or, occasionally on television. But the Internet has entered the equation and now most publishers have a Web site more or less effectively promoting a particular book or the whole list. The site may also accept on-line sales, though the specialist on-line bookstores are likely to sell a greater numbers of books. However if on-line book selling can work for publishers, what is to stop them going a stage further and setting up branded bookshops in the high street, or more likely, in the airport?

The publisher's rep in 21st century will be rather different from the order taker of today. Neither booksellers nor publishers can afford to retain the *status quo*. As on-going sales details are fed from bookshops to their head office, or direct to publishers, the rep will have access to this sales data and be expected to act on it to work with the bookseller to maximise his company's sales. There will be less emphasis on the List, since that information will have been transmitted digitally to the retail buyers. There will be greater emphasis on training sales staff to respond to their customers.

The digital network will allow almost every aspect of the book to change right up to the moment the printer receives the final data. Reprints, while using the same text, may be otherwise completely different in appearance from the first edition. The process of generating a new cover to tie in with a film or television series will appear crude by comparison. Different editions can be expected for individual bookshops or chains. Books might carry the Waterstone's' imprint and house style, in the same way that own label products flourish in supermarkets.

APPLICATIONS

While magazine publishers have, almost without exception, chosen to work with QuarkXPress as the principal computer application to create their products, the choice among book publishers is much more varied. The problem with Quark has been that it is very much a single page at a time application, whereas with the exception of heavily illustrated books, the requirement is for a software which can handle multiple pages. Indeed the large, purpose-built computer systems designed by Penta, Miles 33 and Interset (the first electronic typesetting systems, pre-dating Quark, large and expensive and possessed by traditional typesetting companies) have existed far longer than they had any right to.

The requirement in the future, if it is not already, will be to support standard open formats and computer systems. It will not matter what computer brand or operating system is used, nor what software application the publisher prefers. The choice of standard format comes down to two – SGML or pdf. The latter takes up after the page has been designed and its key feature is to retain the appearance of that page no matter what is done to it afterwards. The page will appear the same whether printed at low resolution, high resolution or viewed on screen. It is also the format that the printing industry is moving towards to solve problems with digital workflow in their prepress production departments. For printers, the advantage of pdf is that each page has the same file size, so will take a known period of time to process. The individual pages can be moved as required into different impositions to suit different printing presses. However if the publisher wants to change the page orientation or the typefaces, pdf is not a comfortable format to work with.

SGML by contrast labels each element of a document, but does not impose the page appearance, so that editing the text remains possible. It is not an ideal format for the printing industry, but is preferable for publishers wanting to move texts into different styles in order to suit different media. SGML is a format that translates easily to Web display or to CD-ROM. The ideal format will be one that combines the advantages of the two formats. Already there are discussions about how to integrate SGML and pdf, though the former or a derivation of it, will remain favoured by publishers while printers will hold databases in pdf for rapid reprints.

Either way PostScript is on the way out. The format responsible for desktop publishing has lasted more than 15 years, and has been responsible for tasks it was never intended to undertake. Adobe conceived it for office applications, but it has been driven by the printing industry's enthusiasm for a format which could free companies from closed environments and the expense of proprietary systems suppliers. As a format for printing a single page PostScript is fine, but it has struggled when handling large complex pages and has not been able to cope with the demands imposed by completely digital workflows.

Software too is likely to move beyond either Quark or Corel Publisher towards an application that is equally at home working on single or multiple pages, and generating SGML or pdf files. SGML generation has been troublesome as the codes can be intricate and accuracy in keyboarding is essential. The training demands are therefore higher than for the design-led Quark and PageMaker software packages. Newer versions of applications like Advent's 3B2, possibly the most popular SGML authoring software, are already making this process simpler and will lead to SGML authoring software that is as intuitive to use as wordprocessing. Already 3B2 can run through a stream of SGML encoded text and locate the incorrect codes, flagging them for the author to change.

Adobe, the owner of PageMaker, will be instrumental in moving the argument on. It also owns Illustrator, the artwork creation application, Photoshop the creative retouching software and PageMill, a leading software for building Web sites. It is also the originator of pdf and sees its future in driving forward the expansion of the Internet and electronic publishing. It has in development a ground up rewrite of PageMaker, which will take advantage of newer systems for software development and will have an emphasis on more complex longer documents and publishing on multi-media.

The pdf files will transmit directly to printers as required. In most cases however, the files will be held in a database, either one belonging to the printer or one that belongs to the publisher. The ideal database will be one where the publisher holds text as SGML and one where the printer holds pdf. The printer will be expected to call off the book from the publisher's database, the transformation from one format to the other being carried out automatically.

The publisher's network will link in the other direction to booksellers, gathering sales information via Epos and other tracking technologies. The strength of the big combines, WH Smith and Waterstone's in the UK, Barnes & Noble and Borders in the USA, should make it straightforward, since these chains will be collecting the sales information for their internal purposes. Working with the independent sector will be more difficult, but as smaller shops gradually come on-line, it should be possible by the early years of the next century to track sales of every title publishers have on their lists. Decisions about reprints, or deliveries to certain shops will be made from firm information, not guesstimates. Much of the decision making will be left to the system, comparing current trends against historical data.

STRUCTURES

While technology has made it easier for retail chains to operate, digital technology will make it easier for the giant publishers to perform. Financial demands are pushing conglomerates to concentrate on core activities. Where book publishing does not fit, it will be sold. Publishing will be concentrated in fewer, larger hands. These super publishers, perhaps only a handful worldwide, will wield enormous power over their customers and suppliers. The terms of trade which have squeezed the share of a cover price payable to the publisher have made publishing much less lucrative than in the past. Success has proved both expensive or unpredictable (apart from information publishing). Larger companies are better equipped to assume the risks.

At the other end of the scale, digital technology is making it easier for smaller publishers to operate. Many tasks can be carried out around the computer, with more and more of these becoming automated. Experience in editing, design and marketing can be brought in from other small companies. Developments in printing technology mean that it is economic to print only small numbers of any title. Video conferencing and digital communications will take the place of face to face meetings, while the remote printing of page proofs has done away with typesetting and courier costs. These companies will not be able to compete with the behemoth publishers in trade paperbacks, but when it comes to niche markets, small companies will be better able to exploit a gap faster. In any case many of these niche books will be too small attract the attention of the transcontinental publishers.

The Internet will enable the smaller publishers to sell to a worldwide audience without huge expense. In fact the Internet will allow a new breed of self-publisher, controlling their own value. This is beginning to happen already as a result of the huge advances paid by publishers to bankable authors. In the future there will be little to prevent those authors acting as their own publishers. Some, like Timothy Mo, have already done so. Such authors will buy in the skills needed to create, print and distribute their book, leading to the situation where the author pays a fee to the publisher for services rendered – the reverse of what happens now. Where authors are a known quantity, they won't need to start a large company. With print-on-demand production methods for example, there is no need for warehousing. Printers can be expected to take on more of the fulfilment tasks. Many tasks that the publisher has performed over the years can be stripped out, uncovering the core task once again. If larger publishers do not recognise this, there will be plenty of smaller start up operations that will. And thanks to the power of the communications networks, it will not be apparent to the outsider how small a company is. There are no rules which say that a large company has to have a better Web presence than a small company. The future publisher will also be able to form alliances, not just with suppliers across the Net, but with like minded companies on other continents. This could lead to a network of virtual multinationals devoid of the heavy layers of bureaucracy that can deaden innovation.

COPYRIGHT

There are dangers to the Internet however, because it is so simple to give information away – anathema to the publishing industry which exists to sell exclusive information which it protects by means of copyright. Naturally, there are strenuous efforts to control copyright on the Web. The Digital Object Indentifier (DOI) will be universally adopted as the means of giving creative works unique identification numbers. The system builds on existing standards of the International Standard Book Number (ISBN), the International Standard Serial Number (ISSN), a Serial Item Control Identifier (SICI) or perhaps the Publisher Item Identifier (PII), a standard supported by some academic publishers. The idea of the DOI is to give every book, article, image or whatever a publisher decides, a unique number which identifies the registration agency, the registrant, the type of identifier (i.e. the ISBN) and a number to identify the product. The DOIs are held in a data base, with links and references to the copyright holder for that material or item. A researcher or customer coming across the material on the Internet will also find the relevant DOI. This will be linked to the DOI repository, with information about its origins and another link to the copyright holder.

At present the DOI scheme has been proposed in the USA, though not formally adopted. As a result, there is no standard for what information should appear on the DOI form, nor indeed whether the DOI system should stand alone or become part of a wider system. The system originated in the USA where the Association of American Publishers carried out much of the initial work. Its intention was to create 'electronic license plates' for the digital data travelling the information superhighway. RR Bowker, the company maintaining the US Books in Print database and responsible for administering the ISBN Agency in the USA, has taken the work of turning the DOI proposals into a working model which was shown at the 1997 Frankfurt Book Fair. The launch drew a packed audience, learning that the system was now in the hands of a non-profit making organisation called the International DOI Foundation whose purpose 'is to support the needs of the intellectual property community in the digital environment, by establishing and governing the DOI system, setting policies for the system, choosing service providers for the system and overseeing the successful operation of the system'.

The DOI by itself will not solve the problems of maintaining copyright on the Internet. Indeed the whole structure may be on the point of collapse. Technologist and Internet evangelist Esther Dyson has suggested that it is pointless to attempt to retain any copyright control, unless it is through password protected areas on the Web. Even then there is little to protect the copying or retransmission of this data. Publishers will not earn their money through the intellectual property but through the relationships that they can build up with customers and the provision of specialised services.

In the meantime, and for as long as they can continue to do so, publishers will want to transfer the copyright system in the digital medium. The USA has sought to address the issue through a proposed Copyright Act which would be used as the basis for renewed legislation in Europe. This, however, is aimed more at protecting the rights of software developers and offering them protection against the uncontrolled distribution of software over the Web.

Even if such proposals become law, publishers will take control of protecting copyright. The ICL content management system includes copyright control in its suite of applications that are aimed at helping publishers leverage money making opportunities from the Internet. These include control over setting up viable distribution channels, security, narrow casting, rights management, flexible tariffing, demographic information capture and analysis and electronic commerce. Aside from access control using passwords to protect a site, ICL offers encryption and other features to ensure that users reach only those levels they are permitted to access.

In copyright control, ICL has exploited a feature of pdf to allow it to add a grey underprint beneath the text saying 'Do not photocopy' or something similar. ICL goes a stage further by adding a digital stamp to the pdf files to record personal details on the paper at the point of delivery. Each action is logged and therefore can be assigned a value and the customer billed according to use of material.

A number of commercial encryption softwares are also appearing on the market, promising to identify images should they be copied. These digital watermarks are embedded in the image and are invisible to the naked eye. The unique data string is hidden in a part of the image deemed 'noisy' – that is with a lot of extraneous information that does not affect the final appearance of the image. It is harder to hide such a string in a text file, since this has little extraneous information.

Encryption software from Digimarc, Highwater or SysCorp, will become widely used as the number of images on the public networks grows. Their effectiveness remains to be tested, though Graham Manders, marketing director at Highwater in Cheltenham, reckons that extensive and repeated image compression and decompression does not destroy the coding. Highwater intends making the identification software available at little cost, earning revenue from sales of the readers needed to identify its watermarks. But a concern for publishers considering the adoption of one or other watermarking system, is the survival of the system into the future and whether there can be any cross compatibility between the different products on offer.

ELECTRONIC PUBLISHING

The Internet is just one form of electronic publishing and many publishers cannot see it offering a worth-while financial return. In contrast the CD-ROM has proved attractive, not least because the unit cost per title model of charging appears close to that of book publishing. It is not. Many publishers have set up teams to investigate and develop a

CD product, but have found that the existing model does not work and that replicating a printed product in electronic form is not an option. A successful product requires added value, an example being the *Conference Blue and Green Book*, a directory of conference facilities and hotels across the country. In the printed form, the reader can look up the data for one establishment, note it down and compare it with another. In the electronic form, there are sophisticated search facilities providing a number of means to locate a hotel with the right facilities. It also offers virtual images of the chosen establishment so that readers can visit the hotel from their own offices.

CDs have not proved to be the easy money earners that publishers had hoped. But two factors may send them back to CD production. Firstly, the advent of digital variable disks (DVDs) will provide a means of carrying a whole range of digital information – particularly films – since the 4Gb capacity is enough for most feature films. Secondly publishers will learn what works on a CD and will work with outside contractors to help bring products to market. Expected bestselling books will appear with CDs attached, as the John Grisham book *Politika* already has. Here an interactive game is the chosen addition, but the electronic media will also see a self-learn CD as a 'must' to accompany many leisure titles, enhancing the experience for the consumer. Examples might be a cookbook with video snatches, showing in interactive format just how the sauce is prepared, or a fishing title with clips showing how to cast the perfect salmon fly. This is also true in the educational sector where the textbook itself may just be the hub around which spin many more multi-media learning items.

The books most vulnerable to electronic media are naturally the reference titles where digital technology is able to search and sort data in a number of ways. Dictionaries and encyclopaedias will also be cheaper in electronic format as the *Oxford English Dictionary* and various encyclopaedias including *Britannica* have shown. Directories are expected to be even more vulnerable to digital challenge. Well before

2010 the majority of directories will be electronic, creating a problem for publishers used to revenue from cover sales. According to the Electronic Document Systems Foundation in the USA, other sectors will be more or less vulnerable. Trade books will transfer to electronic media 'at a snail's pace'. However it suggests that many conventional publications will be tied in to electronic products – a book with an interactive CD perhaps.

Michael Lynton, chief executive officer of Penguin, agrees that trade books are unlikely to transfer to electronic media, saying that the central problem trade publishers face is how to sell more books, more efficiently. Writing in *The Bookseller*, he has declared: 'Publishers have to appreciate that the scope for imaginative marketing of new books has grown hugely and will go on growing'.

While he believes that books are secure, trade publishers will tend to concentrate on fewer authors in order to maximise their 'hit rate' and will expect to have a high rate of churn, a book having shelf space for only a few months. Internally the publisher has to come to terms with the dearth of editorial talent, a problem exacerbated by low starting salaries. Publishers have tended to exploit the vocational aspect that people entering the business have felt towards books. This is no longer good enough when the stakes are higher and additional skills are required. Salaries will have to rise or the problem will worsen.

The biggest problem that publishers will face in the digital age will be the intense competition for readers' attention. Hundreds of television channels, hologram films and increased opportunities for travel and sport will fight for the citizen's money and time. Books will not disappear, though there will be migration away from paper in some areas. The old clichés – that it is uncomfortable to read a computer screen on a train or plane, that a paper publication is portable, user-friendly and, with the help of a pen, interactive, hold good. Digital age publishers however, will be able to move beyond the confines of the book in order to win the fight for consumers' time and spending power. The need to manage the book creation process will remain, but internally and externally things will look rather different. Publishers that anticipate or can react rapidly to the forces of change will succeed.

❹ Bookselling

THE success of book sales on the Internet has given a clear signal that bookselling is changing. Amazon.com is held up as the perfect commercial Web site and has become the largest bookseller in the world, without having a single physical bookshop. It has spawned a host of imitators including several in the UK. But it is not just the threat from Internet sites that is changing bookselling. Books are for sale everywhere: supermarkets carry fast turnover lines, specialist sports shops carry related titles as do music shops. Children's clothes shops are selling books. It is no accident that Tim Waterstone's latest venture is the Daisy & Tom children's retail chain.

▲   ▲   ▲

Booksellers however have been reluctant to confront the threat. The chains seem unable to change while the independents, either through arrogance or ignorance, appear to be stuck in a different time zone. Few independent shops have even bought computers to link themselves to the Web to see what is out there. Meanwhile an increasing number of publishers and larger bookshops are going on-line, though it is unclear whether these sites exist to generate sales independently or to promote the traditional method of selling.

DIGITAL ORDERING

In one sense, booksellers have been part of a digital chain for years. The ISBN system of assigning individual numbers to every book available, is an essential building brick in a digital chain identifying every book published. It allows the bookseller to order books and the wholesaler and publisher to track sales.

Together with the bar code, it has formed the basis for electronic point of sale systems and data tracking systems. However this is as far as it goes. The Booksellers Association (BA) reckons that just half of UK booksellers are using some kind of automated ordering system. But the take up rate is growing fast and within a few years all but the die hard booksellers will have acquired computers for on-line ordering purposes. The number of booksellers installing computers to demonstrate multi-media products is also growing quickly, even if penetration is still only 15 per cent of the market. Of the BA members, 16 per cent have access to the Internet while just six per cent have established a Web site.

In the future the Internet and tele-ordering are going to be the very stuff of bookselling, while sales of the CD, or its successor the DVD could yet revive to the sorts of levels once dreamed of.

So far however, few booksellers and few publishers have begun to grasp the potential for digital ordering. An exception, and a model for others to follow, is Macmillan Distribution Ltd (MDL). It has designed a Web site for exclusive use by the book trade. The bookseller can use a standard Web interface to access the MDL database and search for information on price and availability of each title. The same interface can be used to place orders and then to track the progress of that order. Invoices and delivery notes will be generated automatically and sent to the appropriate computers.

This system will become universally accepted over the next decade, including all publishers and booksellers in a network that will reduce costs on all sides and eliminate errors based on misunderstandings and human error. The computer network will of course be open round the clock, eliminating the pressure to call in orders before the office closes and leaving the bookseller free to maximise his shop floor hours.

MARKETING

By the next century, the trade Web sites will be encouraging booksellers to order copies of the forthcoming blockbuster in advance. They will show cover designs and provide marketing material that can be downloaded and used for in-store displays. These displays may be printed, but may also use digital imagery or video and sound. Large flat panel monitors will certainly be used in other retail outlets. Bookshops will be no different.

This is just a start. The successful bookshop of the next century will not be able to rely on passing trade to generate sales. There will be more pro-active marketing, using demographic information and databases built from the profiles of the customers that use the store. If a customer has, on previous visits, bought a number of John Grisham books, the chances are good that the same customer will want the new title from the same author. A swift mail shot to this customer, produced on a digital printing press, using its variable information potential to match title to potential customer, will increase the chance of a future sale. Publishers will have to co-operate with this effort, providing the digital template for the mail shot to which the bookseller adds the personalised customer data.

Even a simple newsletter to a mailing list of customers will improve the links between retailer and customer and help establish what is called 'relationship marketing' – predicted to be very big in the next decade. But relationship marketing is only going to be possible through the accumulation of information about customers that can be stored in a database. This lies behind the loyalty card schemes that high street supermarkets are running. The aim is to obtain as much information about a consumer's buying habits as possible and then to use the information to encourage further sales. The rationale is that customers will respond to precise and useful information rather than to a random piece of junk mail.

A stage further will move the information from a targeted letter to a digital message, sent as an e-mail to the targeted customer who may be able to reserve or purchase the book. The bookseller is actively going to the customer to make a sale rather than waiting for the customer to come by.

BOOKSHOPS OF THE FUTURE

When that customer does come by, tomorrow's bookshop will be rather different to today's. The US giants, likes Borders and Barnes & Noble, have blazed a trail, making book purchasing a far more enjoyable process. The methods they have pioneered have been imitated by numerous US independents. These are generally massive stores spread over several levels, light and airy, with music, a selection of magazines and multi-media available alongside the books. There are areas to read and often a coffee bar. (The coffee is generally real, as opposed to the frothy heated flavoured milk that is sold by West Coast coffee franchises.) Customers are encouraged to sit and read as much as to buy. It is the absolute opposite to UK super stores like Foyles, which seem to revel in their traditional bookishness and can be off-putting to all but the most dedicated purchaser.

This US style of retailing is going to come to the UK. In 1997 Borders paid £40m for the UK group Books Etc.. Although it has pledged to retain the Books Etc. brand, the urge to have a world brand will sooner or later push the UK name to the background. Barnes & Noble is also looking at moving into the UK – moves which will leave the UK chains vulnerable to the massive resources that these companies can command. The typical Borders shop has something between

125,000-150,000 books, 75,000 music CDs and non-book products, arranged over 35,000 sq. ft. of sales space.

Among the resources such chains can call on are detailed information systems for tracking sales and ordering stock from its own warehouses and from publishers. The publishers, who have been driving down the number of suppliers they use, will welcome the development of fewer relationships on the sales side.

INTERNET BOOKSELLERS

Yet even the size of Borders and Barnes & Noble is dwarfed by the Internet booksellers. Despite a large number of newer cyberstores, including Barnes & Noble, Amazon.com remains the largest and the pacesetter. It is early days still for sales over the Internet. Research from consultancy group CAP Gemini indicates that retailers expect electronic shopping to increase by 26 per cent over the next decade, culminating in a figure of 14 per cent of total retail sales generated by the Internet. However booksellers expect that their trade will be affected by a greater swing than this, given that books are a known entity and there is little risk involved in buying on-line, not always the case with some consumer durables, like clothes.

In 1996 Amazon.com earned sales of £9.6m – not much compared to regular book sellers. But growth is exponential. It sold its first book in July 1995. In 1996 it dealt with 180,000 customers. Penguin reckons that its sales through Amazon.com are growing at 40 per cent a quarter and Amazon.com will soon become Penguin's largest single customer. Amazon.com has almost instant access to 2.5 million titles and because it has no retail overhead it can afford to discount best selling titles by 40 per cent.

Amazon.com was started by a former Wall Street financier Jeff Bezos, who analysed 20 market segments to decide which would be the most suitable for the Internet. Books came out on top. "There are many more items in the book field and there's unlimited shelf space on-line. Maybe there are three million book titles world-wide, whereas in music there are maybe 300,000. I believe the Internet is under-hyped. In the future we're going to have books finding readers rather than readers finding books."

One way this is happening is through links from other Internet sites to the Amazon.com pages. A Web surfer looking at a sports site may be invited to click the link to Amazon.com in order to buy books about the subject. Everyone wins. Amazon.com receives more visitors, the host site adds value and interest to his Web pages and the visitor is presented with additional options.

The site itself operates as much like a bookshop as it can. There is a literary newsletter, interviews with authors, extracts from books reviews and, importantly, reviews submitted by members of the public. It is creating the ambience of a book lovers club. Search engines can locate the books held and off-site searches can be carried out for books that have gone out of print. In future, digital printing units either owned by Amazon.com or contracted to it, will produce these out of print titles on demand. Books will no longer be out of print or out of stock – something with wide implications for the whole book trade. The Internet site is developing constantly and as the technology driving the Internet itself continues to expand and mature, Amazon.com can confidently be expected to add additional features and services. Video clips, on-line conference presentations, readings by authors, are all within the realm of possibility. As Amazon.com adds other products, music and videos for example, these features become intrinsic to the business. And since usage and understanding of the Internet is still well below the levels it will reach, the financiers backing Amazon.com are confident they will receive a healthy return on their investment.

Publishers too will use the multi-media power of the Internet to create the mystique around a title that jump starts sales. America Online has previewed novels by Tom Clancy and John Grisham before their full launch. For the launch of Tom Clancy's novel *Power Plays: Politika*, AOL members were invited to read the first two chapters six days ahead of the official launch. There was an on-line discussion with the author and the novel itself, with an initial print run of 1.6 million copies, came with a free CD-Rom branded as *Tom Clancy's Politika*.

This sort of marketing is closer to the movie business and is sure to continue either on publishers' Web sites, the 'networks' owned by AOL or the Microsoft Network, or through the likes of Amazon.com.

Electronic shopping developments are not confined to North America, although US companies have probably around a year's more experience. Book Data is a UK company building a Web site to hold 'the largest volume of quality information on English language books in print on the Interrnet'. As a paper based company, it is already among the largest providers of bibliographic information, much of which will be held in databases. Making this available electronically is not therefore a case of re-engineering the entire operation. Its database is a natural for the Internet. It offers user-friendly, clear and detailed descriptions of books available. The Web site is being launched as The Book Place – the on-line manifestation of Book Data. It will be able to sell books via a number of partnerships, but its more important role will be in providing information to independent booksellers.

These will be able to access Book Data's bibliographic database through their individual Web sites or home pages. As far as the book buying customer is aware, the information is presented under the supplier's interface as the local bookshop on-line, continuing the relationship between retailer and customer into the electronic medium. A second bookseller may be drawing from the same data well, but because the user interface is different, this will not be apparent to the book buyer.

At its peak, the volume of requests and transactions is expected to be beyond the capabilities of a simple server. This too will provide a reason for the site's success, since it will be far more robust than a bookshop renting space on a site provided by an Internet Service Provider that does not have the power to handle the traffic generated.

Amazon.com was not the first to offer books on the Internet. That distinction probably belongs to Open Communications, which specialises in computer books and has around 11,000 titles available. It was set up with around $1,000 of capital, demonstrating two features of Internet book selling. Firstly there are no massive overheads in premises, stock and staff. This will have important implications if traditional book outlets attempt to compete on price. They cannot.

Secondly the specialist nature of the titles that Open Communications sells will be a feature of many Internet sites. In this way mail order book selling is reaching a much wider audience and with less cost, since the customer comes to the virtual bookshop rather than having to be sent a periodic stock list. Equally, for mail order to work, the retailer needs to know the customer and have details stored on a mailing list. This is clearly not the case on the Internet, though the address will be captured once the customer has responded.

As already noted, the price of a book sold over the Internet can be much lower than one sold through a main street book store or one of the super stores located in shopping centres. Certainly the high rentals charged for the major out of town malls in the UK are a massive disincentive to any but the largest retailers. Even these will find that, although the stores are busier, the overhead is steeper. There is no rental on the Internet other than a small charge to maintain the Web site. However the importance of maintenance is crucial, as Amazon.com discovered when its site failed for the best part of a day!

Internet booksellers are beginning to exploit their advantage in terms of pricing, with increasing levels of discount being offered on the fastest moving titles. Amazon.com has given discounts of as much as 40 per cent on its top 500 titles. The impact of this is increased because there are no local sales taxes to pay to the state governments in the USA.

The global nature of the Internet is creating a new set of challenges that did not exist before, except on the smallest of scales, namely cross border transactions. Amazon.com is already dealing with European and especially UK based customers, opening up potential problems that have existed in isolation before. UK sites are deriving as much as 80 per cent of their business from overseas. Outright book bans of the type imposed on *Spycatcher* will be impossible in a world where it is bits and bytes and not atoms that travel the globe – as Nicholas Negroponte of the Massachusetts Institute of Technology would have it. Publishers are at present attempting to make a stand against certain international sales and have shown that this is possible in the case of the Kitty Kelley book on the royal family. The US book sites managed to restrict sales coming from the UK. However demand was not huge, so there was little pressure to challenge the system and it was not too expensive for the cyber book stores to cooperate.

The issue is one of copyright, where the rights to a book have been sold to a UK based publisher and to a different US publisher. A book delivered to a UK customer from a US Web site stands in contravention of the established trading conventions. However the structure of copyright law will become more difficult to police as increasing amounts of business are carried out over the Web. In the magazine and newspaper world, authors and journalists have woken up to the fact that their work is being distributed electronically without any payment. But it will be almost impossible to control the distribution of such material – including books. Work has been undertaken to try to identify sequences of words, or an encryption key embedded in a text, but there seems little pressure for a change while discussions about policing are still underway.

Mike Shatzkin, founder of the New York consulting firm of Idea Logic Company, has identified minimum requirements for any Internet bookseller. They must offer a complete list of all books in print, relying on the support of the large wholesalers – in the way that Amazon.com works closely with Ingram. Innovations such as foreign language books, or previously owned titles and other areas of special interest, are needed to create a value added reason to use one site rather than another. Sites that are associated with terrestrial book stores need to offer a far greater range of titles than are normally stocked in store. Finally, the experience of the site visit itself will be the key and will need to be welcoming and user-friendly, in the same way that terrestrial stores have found that they had to improve their amenities by offering coffee and a place to sit and read. Some may provide taster chapters of latest titles; or an extended database of books in print with bibliographical information, as the Book Place is able to do; question and answer sessions with authors – anything that recreates the browsing atmosphere that seems crucial to the book buying public.

According to Shatzkin, booksellers will retain their key place in the distribution chain, no matter how hard publishers try to sell direct themselves. Most of the larger US and increasingly UK publishers offer a service selling a promoted book direct from publisher to customer. But they will not take over the role of the bookseller proper as the store is still the gateway dealing with all publishers in one place. In addition, customers may know what book they want, but not who has published it.

Publishers will come to work with Internet booksellers, providing the point of sale advertising that accompanies any major book launch. The sales material will be stored in a sealed site, an FTP site, accessible through a password by the booksellers. They will be able to download images, text and perhaps promotional games to feed their own sites. Interactivity is considered a key feature of the Internet and the ability to engage the surfer is important in enhancing the on-line shopping expedition, the cyberspace equivalent of tropical flowers, waterfalls and benches in the shopping centre.

DISTRIBUTION

Electronic distribution overcomes one of the costliest aspects of the book production process, moving paper from mill to printer and from printer to warehouse, from there to the bookshop and finally to the customer. The customer knows nothing and cares less about the production chain. Her interest is in buying the desired book at the right price. The publisher on the other hand wants to produce the precise number of books that will be sold in a given time in order to control costs.

Nevertheless even Amazon.com will have to move atoms in the form of books at some point. It, and the other cyberbook stores that follow (and Bezos reckons there will be eventually be just two or three leading players dominating bookselling on the Internet), will have distribution on each continent. These warehouses will hold minimal levels of stock from each publisher, but at least one copy of every book in print throughout the world.

With the UK alone bringing 100,000 new titles and new editions to the market each year, and the USA about 450,000 titles, this makes Amazon.com's intentions a very tall order.

The obvious solution is the print run of one, where the book is only printed when and where it is needed. This could of course be in the home, and certainly the desktop printers available in the home of 2010 will be quite capable of printing books on demand. Being capable however does no mean it will happen. Printing at home will require some kind of 'at home bindery', to fold the sheets and complete the book. Even the most enthusiastic will find home book production at best fiddly. Few printers will be capable of duplex production, that is able to print both sides of the paper simultaneously – as we saw with the *Daily Leyland* in the first chapter. Book printing at home will also be time consuming, expensive in terms of the materials required and will prevent the printer from being used for other, perhaps more fruitful, activities. Home printing of this kind will also require binding systems which are awkward to use and need space and heat to create an efficient bind.

This does not apply to the bookshop. The cost of high speed laser and high quality inkjet printing is falling as the speed of printing is increasing. Web printing means no restriction to the A4 format, nor to the types of paper that can be used. The bookshop can afford to invest in the dedicated digital printing operation with a specialist binding unit and trained operator. This will easily be capable of printing out books on demand on the spot, while the customer waits. More likely still the customer will order the title through a the Web site and pick the book up when passing.

ON-DEMAND COPIES

The technology of digital printing is discussed elsewhere, but it is interesting to note that the major suppliers all consider on-demand book printing to be a massive market over the next decade. They can be seen at major print exhibitions, all demonstrating this capability by printing out on-demand copies of *Alice in Wonderland* with Tenniell's illustrations which happens to be the Adobe provided test file!

For this to happen, publishers will need to create digital databases and make them available to the book producer. Straightforward encryption will defeat piracy and other software will prevent the text from being printed more than the once that is being paid for. The text of books held in a digital database needs to be in a format that the digital press understands and can process rapidly. The Adobe developed Acrobat pdf format offers integrity of design and a small file size for transmission over the Web. However the very integrity is a handicap if the format of the book does not correspond to the format of the digital version. SGML and a number of variants and sub-variants do not have this restriction but may be more difficult to work with.

The problem is that as yet the two formats are incompatible, though support for SGML within pdf is likely – Adobe is not saying when. Publishers however will have to chose to make the digital files that will be sent to the printer for film and plate making, available to booksellers via the Web. In the USA this business model is being tested or is about to be tested in three areas. Some envisage placing the printing operation inside the bookshop, or at least its basement, others envisage putting the print in a separate building with one print operation serving a number of outlets in a satellite operation.

Paying customers will either order their books on a special kiosk in the store and wait for them to be delivered, or place the order using the Internet, via the store's Web site and then come to the store to pick up the finished books.

Customers should in theory choose most of the printing parameters themselves, including typefaces. In reality the choice is likely to be restricted to the page format and the binding. Customers will be able to create libraries of their own bindings or more likely the bookshop will in effect become the printer and publisher of its own brand editions. The huge advantage of this is that a book will never go out of print. Because it can be held in a compact digital form, it will always be possible to print a single copy. Matters become more complicated for heavily illustrated titles where the colour images are demanding of computer space and more difficult to replicate accurately on a digital printing press. A new generation of high speed inkjet printing machines will overcome the quality problem, just as advances in digital compression and increased bandwidth will solve the file size issue.

Who pays for the investment and to operate the machinery is at present a contentious issue. There is little vertical integration within the publishing industry. Indeed publishers have been keen to separate the below stairs production businesses from the editorial offices above. Will the bookshops pay, or the publishers, or the printers as the people with the expertise at putting marks on paper? The ultimate answer is far from certain and will depend on where the printing press is located. The most likely solution is that the printer will initially take responsibility on behalf of a single publisher. This is particularly the case if the digital printing operation is to be a satellite plant serving a number of bookshops. More than one UK printer, specialising in short run digital book printing, has had discussions with publishers to this effect. Until something definite is signed, none is willing to speak openly. However it is clear that digital printing is going to become very important to booksellers as well as publishers.

On the spot digital printing will be attractive to academic and technical publishers, where the relative costs of conventional production and warehousing are highest and therefore the cost per page is high. The standard paperback is cheap to produce and deliver and available in sufficient quantities that it is not attractive to print these digitally on-demand. The technical booksellers will also be dealing with students and libraries where there is an increasing demand for pre-packaged educational material, drawing on a number of digital sources. Thus they are more likely to be the first to install the digital laser printers and other printing devices necessary to output digital files.

But where the specialist booksellers go first, others will surely follow. The bookseller of the 21st century will be operating in a completely different way to the bookseller of today.

❺ Academic and Professional Publishing

THE world of academic and professional books is the publishing sector perhaps the most vulnerable to changes in the digital era. The academic journal will be fortunate to last out the twentieth century as a printed paper product. The hold that print has had on the publishing of academic journals and technical and professional publications is already being loosened. Before the next century is too many years old print will account for only a minority of the books being published.

▲   ▲   ▲

These publications are vulnerable to the impact of the digital revolution for a number of reasons: the titles have a high value, often determined by timeliness; they have a limited circulation which can be spread across the country or the world; relatively large numbers of people may want access to them.

Already a number of publishers are working at making their academic journals available via the Internet; others are working towards CD-ROM publishing; others are using electronic collation and digital printing to produce customised publications to suit the subscriber. The academic and professional market is also the first target of two entirely new technologies, the electronic book and bookshops offering on-demand printing.

However not all publishers are welcoming these changes. The small number of publishers operating in this area can be exceedingly profitable and it has been difficult for new publishers to emerge – oparticularly in the field of academic journal publishing. The papers published are supplied at very small cost and the subscribers pay in advance. It is an ideal business, as Robert Maxwell discovered when starting Pergamon Press, and it is therefore not surprising if publishers want to retain as much of it as possible. Indeed the handful of publishers in this area have been concentrating on consolidating their status. Reed's deals with Elsevier, Lexis-Nexis and its attempt on Kluwer, have been driven by this desire. While they are showing interest in the impact that digital technology will have, they are also proving reluctant to take the plunge themselves.

Academic journals have long been produced in SGML, the standardised general mark up language developed to ensure that corporate documents can be transferred electronically. Simple codes are used to identify and distinguish elements in a text, such as body matter, headlines, footnotes, different paragraph styles and so forth. A header file, a DTD (document type definition), is used to ascribe values to each of the standard elements. Through this the elements can be styled to suit the publication. The editors need to know nothing about typesetting structures. That is left to the printer. The same set of codes can be used to transcribe the digital manuscript into an electronic format. Today's basic Internet language, the hypertext mark up language, HTML, is in essence a sub set of the more comprehensive SGML. HTML however, is unlikely to last for anything but the most basic documents shown on screen. More heavily designed magazines and pages will exploit standard formats like XML (extensible mark-up language) and XSL (extensible style language) which have been developed since the advent of the World

Wide Web (see Chapter 2).

The academic publication however does not as yet require these embellishments. The subscribers are not expecting a high standard of presentation and do not seem to require the level of design of a consumer magazine. If presented with a more sophisticated design readers would probably be suspicious rather than delighted. The requirement is for a consistent quality of content and once that is achieved, retaining subscriptions is almost automatic. This in turn helps to make it difficult for new journals to launch against established titles.

Publishers will have a stable of journals and will impose a standard house style, which is far more consistent than in magazine publishing where the drive is to distinguish competing products on a newsagent's shelf. This has brought production savings where a printer can batch a number of titles together on a printing press or at the very least on a binding line.

The production process has been at the least partially digital for a long time. The original material is produced on computer, edited on computer, stored in a digital database, (though not always the publisher's), and increasingly it is printed digitally. Printers have moved from hand assembly of films, to output of partially and then completely imposed pages to film – and frequently to a polyester plate. But it is unlikely that this will satisfy publishers' demands for faster turn round, shorter runs and lower prices even in the medium run.

One feature of Adobe Acrobat, the application that generates pdf files, is its ability to annotate documents, without editing the actual text. This becomes the perfect application for working on academic material, especially for students who can annotate the texts they are working with.

High speed laser printers, evolved from enterprise printers from the likes of Siemens, Océ and IBM and Xerox's DocuTech, are going to wipe away the need for conventional printing. Adobe's Extreme Rip (Raster Image Processor) technology is designed with these printing engines in mind, with speeds up to 1,000pp a minute already within its grasp. The Rip controls the laser as it moves across the film or paper writing the image. The 'raster' refers to the way the laser writes in lines, being turned on and off as necessary. The image is what is created and the processor what is needed to make it work. Before Rips, light was passed through a mask to image a character on the film and typefaces came in what were, effecively, stencil strips or wheels.

The Extreme Rip achieves this phenomenal throughput by first of all creating pdf files from incoming PostScript. The files are very much neater and tidier than PostScript files which can be multi-layered to such an extent that a single file can take an inordinately long time to interpret, while the following file can be processed in seconds. All pdf files are the same size, providing a degree of predictability when it comes to printing. The Extreme Rip uses this feature to split the processing of a document between a number of Rips acting in parallel. The more Rips there are, the faster the potential for printing. Once these devices reach 1,000pp a minute they start to compete with conventional offset in terms of sheer productivity, as well as being able to print each successive page differently. Offset printing is being squeezed out of this market sector.

ON-DEMAND PRINTING

Anthony Rowe, a specialist in short run book printing, became interested in the potential of non impact printing early on, when print runs for academic books became shorter and shorter while at the same time demand for rapid reprints of any single volume grew. It first installed a Xerox DocuTech in 1991, shortly after the machine's launch and now has a number of sheetfed Xerox machines and a reelfed printer from Océ. The company's philosophy is summed up by managing director Ralph Bell: "The inability to produce books at very short runs creates a situation which not only leaves customers dissatisfied, but also poses a real danger to the publisher that a book will go out of print. When this happens, the publication is lost from the publisher's list as the copyright reverts back to the original author. It becomes more than a cost issue. It can directly affect publishers' current and future revenue streams."

For Anthony Rowe reprints are in batches of ten, but in all probability publisher demand will force this lower and the capability exists for single copies to be printed and dispatched. As a consequence of this development, the printer has had to invest heavily in digital databases to store prepared texts and allow for receipt of copy as PostScript files. Equally publishers will need to hold files in a digital print-ready format, with pdf the most suitable candidate for the task. It would then become a simple matter to transfer a complete book over a digital communications link from publisher to printer. Indeed within an intranet, the customer and supplier will be linked to the extent that although the printer is in Chichester and publisher in London, the two appear to be on the same network.

A stage beyond the work that Anthony Rowe is engaged in, is placing the printing system even closer to the point of need. A number of established printers are thinking about how to achieve this. One concept that has been ruled out is that promoted by RR Donnelley, the largest printer in the world. It set up a specialist digital printing operation in Atlanta, close to the airport, which is the main base for the FedEx courier company. The plan was to send files digitally to this facility, print what was required and use the services of FedEx for delivery to the customer. It did not work, and now Donnelley's conventional print plants have digital printing included. Digital printing has to be close to the customer.

A US start up company called Sprout has taken this even further. It has already begun installing printing devices in book stores in the USA. The concept is simple. The store no longer needs to hold as great a range of stock and can be sure that nothing will go out of print. The customer can browse for the title required via a kiosk and order it on screen. The interface on the monitor has been designed to replicate the book hunting experience as closely as possible. Sprout calls it electronic touchability. A few minutes later the book is printed and the store has a sale.

Henry Topping is the driving force behind Sprout and sees numerous stores taking the system. By the end of 1998, there will be 25 outlets with the Sprout equipment and the potential, he claims, is enormous. "It's a question of economics of any particular title. What may be available in the USA is not always available overseas while the language of academic publishing is English and huge demand exists in places like India and other developing countries."

The academic book is deemed most suitable because of its high value per page, where the higher costs of production are mitigated by the greater availability of what will be a limited circulation title. The printing technology used is a mono laser printer twinned with a colour printer to produce covers or illustrations. This can be switched as newer technologies become available. The cutting and binding process has been simplified, so that minimally trained bookstore staff can handle the only manual stage in the production process. "It's as simple as making a Latte (coffee)," Mr Topping declares. It also needs to come close to the quality of existing binding processes because the convenience of being able to produce a book on demand will be outweighed by the inconvenience of a book that spills its pages because the binding is not strong enough. Nevertheless Sprout is an indication of where the academic book market is heading in the next century. If Sprout itself does not make it work, others may pick up the baton.

Sprout will hold the titles on a central database, transferring the digital files to the stores as required. Another option would be for Sprout to receive the call for a title, and to take that book direct from the publisher's database. The Internet is the vehicle for this communication. In tests the actual printing and production process takes around 15 minutes with today's technology, depending on the size of the book itself. Newer systems are certain to reduce that, though the slight delay can provide the store with an opportunity to sell the customer a coffee or snack if nothing else.

The benefits of this method of production seem clear. The store does not need to tie money up in ordering stock, the publisher does not need to print and store titles, there is no risk of losing a sale because a book is out of print, indeed a title now need never be out of print; customers are sure to receive the book they want, however obscure. The drawbacks relate to the initial cost of the Sprout equipment, which will naturally demand a certain rate of usage, and the availability of the titles in database to make the scheme work. This is another reason why the limited world of academic publishing is considered the most logical to start with.

Publishers are reluctant to hand over control of their material at present. "It's a question of just getting them to move a little," Mr Topping explains. "We need to create in their minds our vision of the world. People buy books one at a time. It therefore make sense economically that they now have the ability to sell one at a time. The publisher is selling information and given that, we are not so sure that selling books the current way is the best way."

So the Sprout technology will not be restricted to book stores, but will appear in cybercafes or most likely on some university and college campuses. For the publisher, there is the further lure of being able to generate sales abroad by shipping in a digital format rather than hard copy, doing so instantly and avoiding tariff barriers and shipping costs.

CUSTOMISED TEACHING PACKS

Sprout's on-demand printing concept is not new. It is just that the technology now makes it feasible. Less than a decade ago, the world's largest printer RR Donnelley, McGraw-Hill as the publisher and AM

Graphics as equipment supplier teamed up to produce a books-on-demand concept, aimed at the US college market. A digital printing machine, the Electrobook Press was designed and built. This could print at an acceptable speed, varying each successive page so that a complete book could be printed in one pass. Because it was a web press, it could print on both sides of a sheet simultaneously, making a great leap forward in terms of productivity over sheetfed laser copiers.

The technology was better than photocopying or laser printing of the time, since it used a liquid 'electronic ink' rather than toner particles which were large and liable to flake off the paper. The quality of printing the Electrobook produced was certainly acceptable. However the experiment failed. The publisher considered that digital production was to be used for designing customised college books, pulling texts from its Primis database. Quality and speed were improved over copiers and because the books were generated electronically a copier operator was not needed.

It was intended that students 'only pay for the texts they need' and the book would be tailored to suit a particular course of study. However the printing machines were not located on campus but at a special site in Virginia, though called the Books-on-Demand plant. It was books-on-demand, but with a short delay for delivery.

The system failed, partly because the technology was not ready and AM did not have the financial resources to perfect the machine. It also required tutors to select the papers for the book at the start of a semester or college year, which required a change of culture, and thirdly the database was limited to the, albeit vast, range of McGraw-Hill published material. Users cannot be expected to adjust to suit the technology if there are no real benefits to changing.

Technology has now caught up and allows the production to be brought to the point of use. The Primis service is now geared around a custom publishing service operating from the company's Web site. At present this comprises just the Primis catalogues, but will contain additional text material once a way can be found to offer copyright protection. The database contains 150,000 pages of material and is available at 1,500 US education institutions before the move to the Web.

The material remains a mix of lecturers' notes, teaching materials and papers written for the database. The instructor building the course book chooses the material, checks a proof and orders the requisite number. These are delivered from the offsite print operation a week to ten days later. The future, though, will mean the delivery of a pdf version of the material and a licence to print the number agreed on the university campus. The material on the database is all controlled by McGraw Hill, avoiding copyright difficulties. This situation will change in coming years as colleges will want a unified operation rather than having individual publishers offer their own lists exclusively.

There remains a cultural barrier, both among students and publishers. One lecturer reported the reaction from students towards the customised Primis book as follows: "Some students find it difficult, others students say they like the texts because they take a more active role in the learning process." Publishers will surely come to shed their reluctance to abandon control over the number of journals printed in favour of allowing the user to decide.

Awarenesss of these developments is increasing slowly. A recent survey of eight universities found a quarter of the teaching staff were putting together computer based learning materials. And the interest in specialist 'courseware' for students is high. Bill Gates foresees students using such software to test themselves in maths, receiving and filing coursework through the network.

There's no doubt that the barriers preventing the delivery of customised teaching packs are rapidly disappearing. Trials are underway in Scotland to create customised course packs. The Scottish Collaborative On-demand Publishing Enterprise has grown out of a 1993 report looking at the impact of new technology on academic libraries. SCOPE is one of a number of projects looking at the issue under the auspices of eLib, the electronic libraries programme. SCOPE is the project headed by the University of Scotland and it includes 13 higher education institutions connected on the JANET, Joint Academic Network. The aim was to develop a digital resource of academic material that could be used to customise course packs for students and further to develop print-on-demand services to allow printing of academic material at the behest of the reader.

COPYRIGHT

Crucial to the project has been an electronic copyright management system called Cactus. It offers view only, and view and print levels of transaction. Since the material is held in pdf, viewing is possible with a freely distributed Acrobat reader. To print as well, the SCOPE Acrobat Module must be added. The reader selects from titles or chapters on a Web page, from a number of course choices or a search engine. The initial search locates a document and includes the link to the pdf version of the document. Before receiving the document however, the reader must complete a form including password authorisation to use the system. The information gathered will be used to compile transaction reports and track system usage (and misuse). The password may allow the document to be printed and if so, the user's name and time of printing is automatically added to the print-out, as is a security watermark to prevent further copying.

The initial trials have been successful enough for the partners, together with publishers and other institutions to bid to set a national database of digital copyright material. This could set about making the printed versions of journals redundant. However such developments are still in the early stages and there are cultural as well as technical hurdles to overcome. Separate deals need to be struck with the individual copyright holders and payment rates agreed. The Publishers'

Association has suggested 5p a page, SCOPE has struck deals at 2.5p a page. Publishers however remain fearful that any electronic usage will diminish conventional sales. One publisher has agreed to license materials with the qualification that every request will be determined by its impact on sales of the printed version in that particular institution. This reaction will disappear as those publishers who are relaxed about electronic dissemination and print-on-demand are seen to be more successful as a result. If nothing else, as distance learning becomes more acceptable, electronic publishing becomes the only practical way to keep up with technical and academic material.

Schemes like SCOPE should be attractive in that they promote the existing system of editorial control over publication by the publishers. It should allow for a relatively smooth transition into the digital world. However SCOPE has found that certain of its course packs will contain material from individual lecturers, not controlled by professional publishers. It is only a small step from this to the university's own staff providing academic papers to the digital database, placing in jeopardy the existing publisher-journal-paper axis. The risk for publishers is not just a loss of revenue from electronic publishing, but that the education institutions will become their own publishers. If revenue can be earned in this way, few chancellors would baulk at the prospect, particularly with pressure to maximise revenues to the university.

For the moment, it is publishers like Academic Press, a subsidiary of Harcourt Brace, that are leading the way in delivering academic journals electronically. Its massive operation has been set up with software supplied by ICL, whose Commands application is aimed at managing huge volumes of data. Institutions across the world purchase a site licence, allowing access to the International Digital Electronic Access Library (IDEAL). With this and the passwords used to access the journals held in the database, students and tutors can reach the pdf versions of 175 journals, wherever they may be on the licensed network.

THE INTERNET

Academic Press went live on the Internet early in 1995 and it has grown rapidly since. Chris Gibson, head of Electronic Publishing for the publisher in London, said that the volume of information and potential users indicated that outside expertise was required. "Putting 100 pages on the Web was OK, but we needed to publish 25,000 papers a year. The numbers are huge. It was an industrial scale problem and we needed an industrial strength solution. It wasn't just the volume. We needed high reliability, manageable security, wide bandwidth to cope with graphics, video and sound, a large scale database, powerful search facilities and large scale loading capability." The result was the decision to install a complete solution from ICL rather than attempt to build a system from scratch. The demands on such a system go beyond merely providing a database which has a search engine and can retrieve copies of relevant papers.

For Academic Press the system chosen "could manage subscriptions and delegate responsibility for administration to client organisations. This would help keep down the cost of the service and make it more manageable. ICL Commands gave us the freedom to exploit our data in the most appropriate way as the market develops," says Mr Gibson.

There are two sites, one for the USA and a mirror site based in Bath. The number of institutions served keeps growing, but it is unclear as yet exactly who is using the service and their feelings towards it.

IDEAL is not the only on-line service that Academic Press is involved with. It works with others like PubMed in a joint arrangement to make relevant journals available to a select audience. The links that have been built in allow a user to switch from one service to the other instantly. The software will carry out the appropriate checks to ensure that a user has the licence to use the IDEAL service.

PubMed receives texts as SGML documents, allowing these to become available on the service almost instantly. There is in effect no delay before publications are available on the electronic service.

Academic Press is not alone. Dual publishing will be common for a number of years hence, but with the print element diminishing in importance. This will impact on university and college libraries, which will themselves have to move onto the network to supplement their physical existence as repositories of books and places of study. With journals being available on-line, a student need never set foot inside the library proper. The libraries have begun to realise there is a need for cultural change. There is also the changing demographic profile of the student population. Many students will have some kind of job in order to help fund tuition fees and living expenses, restricting the time that can be spent in the library.

The on-line journal need not be restricted to the delivery of words on paper in the way the print product must. Chemical structures can be shown as 3-D objects on a computer screen, medical images will be enhanced.

ON-LINE SERVICES

The opportunities opened by this sort of technology will also forge new alliances to exploit the developing market. In an instance of this, Dow Jones, publisher of the *Wall Street Journal* and other financial information, has come together with academic journal publisher UMI in an agreement to share each other's material on their on-line services. UMI will be able to distribute the content of Dow's print publications while Dow Jones gains access to the text and images published by UMI. The alliance builds on previous links between the two which had earlier led to the publication of Dow Jones information on CD-ROM. According to Ken Tillman senior vice president.: "Nothing stands still. I know access to this on-line content will be well received by our customers who need this type of information for purposes ranging from a presentation to a group, to writing a dissertation or thesis."

There is an increasing number of on-line data bases with search engines that promise instant access. Those that have not moved onto the Internet will do so, because access through the Web browser is infinitely easier than through the individual interfaces that the on-line services provide. For instance SilverPlatter's Search by Search is being used by Reed Elsevier to handle the registration, authorisation, metering and payment processing to open up a pay-by-use service, the most popular concept for earning revenue from on-line journals. SilverPlatter Information, as its name suggests, started out in the CD-ROM market, moving into on-line as demand has grown. Another part of Reed Elsevier, legal publisher Lexis-Nexis, is also providing material over the Web, a move declared to be as revolutionary as the launch of the on-line Lexis service in 1973. The launch of the Lexis-Nexis Xchange Research service was greeted ecstatically. Associate Dean at Yale, Carroll Stevens declared: "This is exactly the direction in which on-line research should be headed. It's a godsend for legal education. We get not only an imaginatively expanded library of resources, but the ease and convenience of a browser to boot."

There are some distinct advantages to screen based publication for many of these titles. The amount of information in printed form concerning the maintenance of a Boeing 747 is such that it could not all fit inside the aircraft. The engineer, armed with a portable PC and manual on CD-ROM, can take the information right up the place of work. All the documentation associated with the development of the Boeing 777 was generated digitally. What is used on civilian and military aircraft today will be used for commercial vehicles in the near future. The home workshop manual that describes how to remove the carburettor is ideal for transposition into a CD or on-line format.

Digital publication offers some crucial advantages to this market, impossible to paper based products. Any updates can be made instantly with the certain knowledge that all subscribers will be accessing the latest version of the data. Hybrid publications that involve an amalgam of data stored on a disk, data that is held in a central server and data that is delivered over the Internet, have enormous potential.

DATABASE RETRIEVAL

Not all digital publication needs to be on screen however. Already in the USA, legal publishers are keeping subscribing attorneys up to date in their particular area of the law by manipulating databases to match a subscriber's interest with the mass of case law that the courts generate. The case reports are created and published in a pdf format and stored in a database. Software from Cascade Systems calls up the articles required and matches the reports with the subscriber profile. The required files are then sent to a digital press which prints only those pages that each subscriber needs. Previously, to carry out this task has meant printing multiple copies of each page, storing them in piles and having an army of manual workers pick the papers from the required stacks to create the publication the subscriber wants.

The new way of working is faster, since there is no time lag between the authoring and printing of an article and its dissemination; it is more efficient to the publisher since only those pages that are needed are printed and it is better for the subscriber since he or she receives the targeted information. The system as it stands uses a central printing operation. The future will see this change to one where the printing engine is based closer to the user. Desktop and network printing will become the norm for many corporate documents including this type of publication.

The information is sent over the Net to the most suitable printing engine closest to the subscriber's desk and either generated overnight or printed as the user wants. Printing will be an option. The information could remain on screen only, but for many publications, legal titles included, the integrity of the content is crucial, so a hard copy of some sort is needed to help prevent any editing by the recipient.

The West is not alone in taking to distributed print-on-demand. IBM Printing Systems is working with the Beijing University research and publishing spin off, the Founder group. Its FIT software is a non-Roman page make up system and is used by the major Chinese publishers and others throughout Asia. IBM secured the rights to market the software, aiming to team it with its Infoprint 4000 high speed black and white laser printer. Founder will put the print-on-demand technology into its network of 30 pre-press operations around China.

In the sphere of academic and professional publishing more than any other, digital publication is not just an alternative to the printed paper version. Digital publishing on the Internet is quite simply the way that these limited circulation, highly specific and information based publications will have to go. The publishers must come up with business models that show revenue from this new form of publishing, concentrating on their role as information providers rather than as distribution operations for printed publications. The industry will not stand still to let those that do not change catch up.

⑥ Magazine Publishing

THE alliance of Apple, Adobe and Aldus in the mid 1980s created desktop publishing and at a stroke made possible the single most revolutionary advance for magazine publishers to date. Typewriters and carbon paper were consigned to the waste bin and hundreds of typesetting companies quickly followed. As a result costs plummeted and it became possible for thousands of new titles to be published.

▲　　▲　　▲

The data processing revolution only touched the editorial desks, and journalists quickly showed their gratitude towards Aldus by preferring the rival page design application called QuarkXPress. There is now scarcely a magazine in the English speaking world that does not use Quark to design and assemble editorial pages.

As the confidence and ambition of users has grown, so too the power of the computers has increased. The innovative designs of *The Face*, *Raygun* and even *Bella* and *Best* would not be possible without Quark. Other applications have played their part, notably Adobe's Photoshop which has become the market leader in colour image composition and retouching on the Apple Mac. Graphics have been created in Illustrator or Freehand. Can these continue to dominate over the next decade?

Perhaps, but they will face an increasing range of challenges, not least from a radically revamped PageMaker product from Adobe. This will be the application that Adobe hopes will last for the next decade and is due to be shown in prototype form before the end of 1998. Its major distinguishing feature is that the new program will be as comfortable producing pages for the Internet as for paper. Electronic publishing and the Internet in particular are going to provide the greatest challenge to magazine publishers, but they need first get to grips with managing their existing operations in the digital era.

Over the last decade, printers have invested millions in highly efficient high speed web offset printing presses which can provide colour anywhere a publisher might wish. This has been aided by rapid developments in scanning, making it possible to produce the colour separations necessary for printing within hours instead of days. Paper mills provided new grades of paper specifically suited to magazine publishing. It added up to a decade when the number of magazines published – business and consumer titles – grew rapidly. During the 1990s the Periodical Publishers' Association, (PPA) the UK publishers' trade body, reckons that magazines were being launched at the rate of one a day. Not all have lasted. However the elimination of typesetting costs and the speed with which magazines can now be put together, has reduced the entry level costs for magazines and encouraged the formation of dozens of new publishing ventures.

Apart from editorial, most parts of the magazine publishing business have, to date, been virtually untouched by digital technology. This is shortly to change and the publishers know it. In 1996, the PPA attracted only a handful of delegates to a conference on the impact of digital change on the production process. A year later the same subject pulled a capacity audience comprising all elements of the production process: editors, production directors, ad managers, repro houses, printers and ad agencies. What caused them anxiety then will have ceased to be a major problem within a few years. In the next century the route to

77

printing will be seamless. Publishers, production houses and printers will be interlinked and once a workflow between the three is agreed, the production process will be as good as automatic. The publisher will drive the system.

This contrasts with the traditional method of putting together a magazine which has come together at the printer. On a light table, a planner, armed with adhesive tape, a scalpel, a stack of film and hard-earned knowledge of the printing process, takes the individual pages and assembles them into a larger film, usually with eight pages positioned so that when folded, each page falls into the correct position. This has to be done accurately to ensure that the colour is printed in register. It is a skilled and labour intensive process and therefore does not fit into a world where speed and economy are prime requirements.

ADVERTISING

Some of the pieces of the jigsaw are in place, some are still missing or not fully formed. The biggest obstacle at the moment is the advertising industry, which is comfortable with the checks and controls that are now in place and fearful that its role will be eliminated by digital technology. However advertising, like the editorial pages, is almost always designed on an Apple Mac. The design will be passed from the ad agency or designer to a professional pre-press operation to carry out the print preparation and to make the films that are sent by motorcycle courier to the printer. This is already unnecessary since digital data can be sent as easily as pieces of film. The objections to change are largely cultural.

The ad agency's client is concerned that all the advertising paid for looks the same, even though it may appear in numerous magazines, printed at several locations and forms part of a campaign involving billboard posters, television ads and product packaging. The agency is paid to oversee quality control and the way it has done so is to produce film and use the film to make a proof which is supposed to act as a faithful rendition of what the printer has to replicate on press. If there is a complaint, the agency is protected by the proof which has been accepted by all parties and is therefore described as a contract proof. Digital working takes the film out of the process so the agency becomes vulnerable. Before a full digital workflow can be accepted, either some form of reliable contract digital proof needs to be developed, or else an acceptable compromise, where not all the printing dots are displayed, is needed.

There are fears that the digital transmission may be corrupted, or that elements of the file may be altered, deliberately or otherwise, by a printer, so destroying the integrity of the ad. As well as a digital proof, the advertising industry therefore requires a file format, which provides the necessary guarantees that there can be no corruption, before there can be widespread adoption of digital transmission.

The first two steps towards this offer apparently contradictory solutions. One is a workable though ultimately cumbersome approach. The other has flaws which will be overcome in the very near future. The US advertising industry, in collaboration with publishers like *Time*, whose production director Frank Scott, has been a major driving force towards the digital future, has come up with an agreed format called TIFF/IT.P1. This is effectively a bitmap format, a digital representation of the separated film needed to make plates and so print with, and is therefore a digital file that is exactly what will be output at the printer. It is unalterable, except for the opportunity to replace some text late at the point of press. The disadvantages of TIFF/IT are this very rigid structure, and also the very large files that the partly processed job creates. It is a solution that exists to solve a problem that publishers have at the turn of the century, but it is also a solution that will not last much beyond the millennium.

In the next century a neater solution will be required. This will almost certainly be a derivation of Adobe's Acrobat portable document format, itself a revised version of PostScript. Adobe originally devised the portable document format as a means of moving documents around corporate computer networks, retaining their integrity on different computer screens and allowing the electronic document to be printed. Adobe considered pdf to be the equivalent of digital paper.

This application did not develop as Adobe had envisaged, but Acrobat has found a new lease of life as a means of displaying publications and pages on the Internet. In another direction, Adobe has also developed pdf as a way of overcoming some of the inconsistencies of PostScript and also as a more compact version of the page description language. As a format for digital ad transmission, pdf will guarantee the integrity of the ad and will be compact enough to send across communication networks. A page that is in this format for printing will also be suitable for publishing on the Web or on a CD-ROM with little alteration.

Creating ads digitally is only part of the puzzle. The responsibility for handling the ad then has to be worked out. In an analog workflow, films arrive at the publisher, are booked in to a production department and will be sent with written instructions to a printer. In a digital workflow, this will be unnecessary. However the magazine's production department will still need to make the decisions on where the ads will be placed. But this will be handled by a computer application. The first versions of these are appearing on the market. The rules they operate to are rudimentary at present and there is little artificial intelligence involved.

The future system will have a sophisticated self-learning feature, which will come to understand the requirements, often different, for each magazine the publisher produces. Late arriving ads, or those booked after the close date, will no longer create mayhem in the production department. The staff will in fact have little idea that a new ad has arrived. It will be sent over the Internet or by some digital link, moving straight to the file server. The set of rules needed to handle the insertion, including multiple dates and special positions, is included and is picked up by the application to give it the indications needed to shuffle the layout and place the new material. Again publishers will continue to hold back from lavishing money on technology. Few applications, in any case, have anything like the sophistication that is needed to handle the production requirements of a magazine publisher with multiple titles.

DIGITAL LINKS

The digital links between agency, publisher and printer will require something more sophisticated than ISDN. Links with greater capacity are becoming available, as are adaptable networks. In the USA, a company called WamNet has exploited what has been an untapped market and has, as a result, seen its customer base explode. In Europe, the running is led by an alliance of Scitex and British Telecom. So far this is only in its infancy, but such networks will become the norm by early in the next century. Each user on the network will pay according to the required capacity and usage of the system. Files, whether image libraries, existing pages or pages in production, will be held in a vast database, partitioned by firewall security to give each client access to their share of the system. It will be straightforward to move files from one client to another, quite unlike the situation now where the ISDN connection is held on one workstation and everything is routed through that. The other drawback with ISDN – that the receiver has to wait until the call is finished before being able to use that line – will also be a thing of the past. For an ISDN user, waiting for an urgent file to arrive, there is nothing worse than having a less vital but lengthy file block the line. In the new communications networks, the recipient can choose to call down the file when it is needed.

British Telecom is backing the establishment of this type of digital network, having earmarked publishing as an industry requiring digital links for large file volumes. However file transfer over the Internet will offer an appealing alternative, especially as the file transfer rates available increase. The networks that the telecommunications service providers can offer must provide something more than merely high speed data links, because otherwise they will lose out as Internet file transfer takes over.

The ease of being able to move files from one place to another will impact on editorial production, linking individual designers and editors with separate pre-press operations, rather than connecting monolithic publishers and printers. Only recently it was considered a matter of time before publishers took control of all their colour scanning needs, a step which would eliminate the need for specialist pre-press companies. IPC led the way in the UK, investing £1m on creating a digital photo library, by transferring the images it held to Kodak Photo CDs and storing these in a massive database managed by specially devised software from The Media Corporation.

However a year after this was officially declared open, IPC stepped back from its declaration, saying that it was inefficient. Nic Bellenberg, who set the system up to a high specification, says the company has found out that outside services are cheaper than trying to handle pre-press within an editorial environment.

THE REPRO HOUSE IN THE DIGITAL AGE

This does not mean that the repro house will continue as it has. It will continue to scan images for a magazine, but will also store the scans in an archive and make this available to its publisher clients. Instead of supplying scanned pictures digitally on a storage medium such as SyQuest or Jaz disks, the scans will be kept in a database which will be open to the customer. The database will be partitioned to allow a magazine access only to its part of the archive. The interface to this collection will be through a Web browser, so it will not matter to the image management company what type of computer the customer has. The designer will call off the low resolution version of the image required when it is required. It will be placed in a page and when this is sent back to the pre-press house, again as a digital file, the print resolution version automatically replaces the placement image. The professional trade house need not be involved in the process in any way.

The transaction will be recorded by the system and a charge levied according to the contract between publisher and supplier. This might be based on the amount of data stored, the time spent accessing it, or the number of images transferred at more than minimum resolution.

The attraction of this way of working lies with the reluctance of publishers to invest in technology that they do not need. One reason for the stagnation of the IPC project is that the suppliers to publishers have made substantial investments in systems and networks and other equipment which a publisher acting alone could not possibly justify. The trade house is also prepared to work round the clock, something that continues to elude the culture of publishing companies.

The price of scanning has fallen and will continue to fall. In a very short time there will be no cost at all to scanning. Charges will only be payable if retouching, storage or other forms of manipulation are required. The quality of simple scanners also increases as ccd (charge coupled device) arrays improve. The drawbacks of the first flatbed scanners using ccd technology are being overcome. The sort of quality that is available only in expensive models from Scitex, Fuji, Screen and the like, will be appearing in desktop scanners from Umax, Hewlett Packard and Agfa before long. Simpler to operate software will undoubtedly arrive, particularly self-adjusting colour management and self-calibration systems, which mean that scanning really does become as straightforward as photocopying. By entering simple job codes, the stored settings for a particular magazine will be called from the network and used to control the scanner. The necessary settings will have been calculated by the printing press, making adjustments for the paper and inks being used. But the number of different parameters that the software has to consider and the amount of information that the processors will have to handle, will make the first artificial intelligence scanners like this affordable only by the professionals – arguably those that need it least.

DIGITAL PHOTOGRAPHY

The distinctions between scanning and digital photography, already fuzzy, is in any case set to disappear. Scanning will be required in order to cope with standing photographic image libraries for many years to come. But digital photography will become more affordable and image libraries are rapidly moving their archives to electronic media, to be made available as CD-ROMs or through Internet sites, rather than expensively printed catalogues. The printed catalogue for these libraries will vanish as the CD, or most probably the Digital Versatile Disk, is cheaper and more convenient. In cases where the same image is wanted by more than one customer, this is possible at no cost. With a library of transparencies, additional duplicates of the original would be necessary, incurring substantial expense.

The appearance of low price, domestic digital cameras, while only suitable for screen reproduction today, will lead to an army of users familiar with digital cameras. Early digital cameras needed to be handled in studio conditions, with long exposures to capture anything like enough information for print purposes. These have been superseded by cameras which can grab enough data in a simple snatched shot, offering the same flexibility as the conventional camera.

Cost and culture have held back the development of digital photography. Photographers with a large investment in conventional equipment are not always keen to replace this collateral, nor to work with a Mac. But fashion shoots will be transformed by digital working, as the processing step is eliminated. Like newspaper photographers, who almost without exception use digital photography, the images from the fashion shoot can be digitally transmitted back to the editorial office. If the pictures are not what is required, the shots can be retaken. The advantage of this is going to be enough to tilt the balance in favour of digital. An acceptable digital camera will quickly become equivalent in price to its film based twin, making the initial step into digital photography less a decision about cost. By early in the next century, the transparency will be more unusual than the disk. Photographers will discover the ease with which their work can be distributed and sold over the Internet, with encryption software taking care of copyright concerns.

Photo libraries have their stock available either on CD or the Internet, while Microsoft chairman Bill Gates, through a related company called Corbis, will have the digital rights to the world's largest collection of images. These images will be delivered on CD-ROM or increasingly over the Web. Current search engines need to trace descriptors to locate an image. If the descriptor is inaccurate, the picture may never be found. Newer search technology will overcome the problems of being able to find images through a description of the outline of its main subject.

Again, military technology is likely to migrate into the civilian arena to offer some help. Avionics software developers are working on ways to identify enemy aircraft or vehicles merely by their shape and with reference to a database. This is intended to lock out weapons systems, so preventing friendly fire incidents. An adaptation of this technology will allow someone looking for an image to sketch an outline, enabling the search software to locate suitable matches for the image within the database. Naturally these digital images are going to be protected by electronic fingerprints in order to prevent copyright fraud. The encryption software uses embedded pieces of digital code that allows a reading program to identify the image even after it has been printed, or has been used in a photomontage to assemble a seemingly new image. The ability to charge small amounts for providing the images will be another step forward, possible thanks to digital technology. Internet image libraries will charge varying amounts for images at different resolutions. The amounts will be relatively small and will be collected automatically. Bill Gates has identified this as having growth potential.

In *The Road Ahead* he writes 'I believe that quality images will be in great demand on the interactive network. My idea that the public will find image-browsing a worth-while pursuit remains to be demonstrated, but I think that with the right interface, the service will appeal to a lot of people. I'm looking forward to being able to ask for 'sailboats' or 'volcanoes' or 'famous scientists' and then seeing what comes up.'

THE PRODUCTION HOUSE

Once the magazine has been pieced together digitally, the story moves on to the production house and the printer. The production house will emerge from the repro house of today. A great many will not be able to make the transition from scanning and producing film or plates. The production house will offer a great many more services, including digital printing, formatting for different types of printing and the handling of digital data. It may also produce separated films or plates, but this task will almost certainly pass to the printer, using digital data supplied by the production house. At present, few magazine printers are able to cope with digital data, or feel comfortable with this way of working. But once a few stumbling blocks have been overcome, the move towards digital output will be swift.

Reluctant as they may be to do so, printers will have to invest in massive databases and the associated software to store and retrieve the editorial and advertising pages. The tools to carry out imposition digitally are being developed and will become completely automatic, driven by a magazine's format and the presses available to print it. To date, imposition has been a slow task and has required all the pages to be in the digital database before it can begin. Few magazines work like this, aiming to keep the possibility of editorial change, or space for a late-arriving ad, open until the last moment. But as pdf workflows, which are based on separate pages rather than on pre-organised sections, come on stream, the system can accept late pages in the same way as conventional workflows allow.

Secondly the power of computer processors will continue to leap forward, moving imposition from being a labour intensive task to a processor based task, and so one without any time penalty. The format of a magazine can therefore be changed right up to the moment that it goes on press, offering savings to both printer and publisher. It will also enable advertisers to design publication-specific ads. To a certain extent this will happen in the newspaper world, where some swift thinking can devise a topical ad to accompany a headline news story. In magazines, the custom ad will be about developing an ad that is specific to the magazine's style and audience. An ad that is suitable for *Woman's Own* will be very different to one in *Cosmopolitan*. More subtly, one that is designed for *FHM* would be different to one appearing in *Loaded*.

At the printer, output will be either to a printing plate generated by a platesetter, or perhaps to a device capable of imaging the plate inside the press. The direct imaging of plates for magazine production is an everyday occurrence in the USA, where there is tighter control of advertising by the publishers. *Time* expects that all advertisements will be supplied digitally, whereas in the UK the ad agency will not trust the publisher to this extent. The US ad is distributed digitally using the TIFF/IT format, which prevents the receiving printer altering the file in any way. It can then be output. Most large circulation weekly magazines in the USA will be printed at a number of plants close to the point of distribution. The USA has also led the way in gathering demographic information about its readers. It is not uncommon for a personalised inkjet printed message to be added to subscription copies of magazines.

SUBSCRIPTIONS

The rate of subscriptions in the USA is far greater than in Europe, helped partly by exceedingly favourable subscription offers. In exchange, the publisher receives a vast amount of demographic information that can be used to sell the publication to advertisers. This is most useful when combined with techniques of Selective or Target binding. The computer is used to decide how a magazine will be made up as it passes along a binding line. Different sections will be relevant to certain readers – sports, gardening, hunting, and so on. The magazine will change to match the profile of the individual reader. Publishers have also taken to surveying news stands to assess which character types are buying their magazine and adjusting the contents of the magazines that the seller receives to match the profile of their readers.

It will be surprising if a European publisher does not attempt to follow the US example. Already, most business magazines operate with controlled circulations in order to give advertisers a defined target market. For a consumer magazine to do likewise will not be a great shock, once the publishers have overcome the problem of cutting the apparent cost of their magazine and therefore appearing to devalue it. In return, the information that is gathered, in terms of profiles of individual subscribers, will be of far greater value in the long term than the cover price revenue. *The Reader's Digest* is a past master at gathering data, though is not always as efficient at using it accurately.

Digest is also a leader in terms of digital production. For many of its editions around the world, a direct digital workflow is now in place. In the UK this means that a production house in south London is used to create the TIFF/IT files which are sent to the printer near Bristol. The last pages can be sent on an ISDN connection, cutting several days from the magazine's production cycle. *Digest* also sends its features out digitally to the separate editorial offices world-wide. They receive the text and the images on CD. As the various editions are made up, the editors can select from the material that comes from the US office, with the owner happy that the correct images have been supplied to suit the articles.

The UK's leading world-wide magazine, *The Economist*, takes a more cautious path at present. It has been transmitting editorial pages to a number of print sites around the globe for some years. Ads however are sent by courier. The publisher continues to use what is in effect a private network to send the pages. Each site has exactly the same equipment, with the same software loaded. The risk is therefore minimised. The format chosen is compressed PostScript, as being the most reliable way of sending. The publisher is now looking at solutions that involve open systems – in other words using a reliable standard format that can be read and understood by a number of imagesetters or platesetters. Pdf will be the way to do this, once some of the issues that relate to production for printing have been addressed.

THE WEB

Of equal concern to *The Economist* and other publishers is the Internet. There is a certain pressure on magazines to move into cyberspace and there are magazines being developed that exploit this new medium. As the capabilities of the World Wide Web become better understood, so more magazines will stake a claim for a presence on the Web or certain magazines may move from an electronic-only presence into one that includes a printed version.

There will be many different ways of going digital. Business magazines will prosper with a site that includes archive material, search engines to access classified and directory information, banded with an up to the minute news service. Consumer magazines may be involved in brand extensions, attempting to recreate the experience of the print magazine on the screen. Odd things happen when a print magazine, which is a spin off of a television programme, moves on to the Internet. The *Road Show* magazine has an Internet site which attempts to capture the spirit of the television broadcast, rather than the print medium. This is part of a much larger BBC Web site, home for the BBC's printed publications. Increasingly, Web sites are going to move beyond the simple few pages into far more complicated entities. It is then that publishers will realise that the capabilities of off-the-shelf applications are no longer enough, and some form of more powerful application will be needed.

This is going to be the case as Web sites, which start as a means of taking a title into the Web, expand into using some of the technologies of the new medium. Magazines of all types will be able to show moving images and, once bandwidth constraints are removed, as they will be within five years, they will. Transactions taking place on the Web will provide a service to readers, a source of revenue to publishers and additional revenue to the client company. It will, in short, be a much more sophisticated version of mail order. A Miller Freeman site called *Dotmusic* is offering a service to allow visitors to buy music CDs through its site, as do many specialist record company sites. In future, customers will be able to buy the music directly from the site and download the selected tracks to their own CDs. *Dotmusic* is the site for the trade magazine *Music Week*. However, the popularity of the site is more with aficionados and fans rather than with those in the business. It's a striking example of how the Internet can break down accepted barriers.

Another Miller Freeman site, *Dotprint*, is trying to take its connections with second hand printing machinery dealers and introduce them to a far wider audience than reads *Printing World*, which has a UK biased circulation. It is also providing an archive of past material, so that readers have a reference library of technical information at the other end of their modems. More and more magazines will strike into the Internet, particularly those that have only a niche circulation at present. For these titles, finding shelf space among the army of titles that major publishers are churning out, is a massive problem. An Internet site overcomes this difficulty to a large extent, so long as the site designer has used meta tags correctly and the site is registered with the requisite number of search engines.

The successful transitions to cyberspace will have to treat the new medium, not as a rival to paper, but as an extension of it. The same rules about attracting loyalty apply, for the site must encourage return visits. And the publisher, if using the site to provide news updates between publication dates (turning a monthly magazine into a news provider), must not allow his bias towards the print publication to strangle development of the electronic version.

However, earning revenue from Web sites is a problem for conventional publishers. To date, few sites have generated anything like sustainable levels of revenue. For a magazine like *The Economist*, dealing in up to the minute analysis, the Internet poses a problem and an opportunity. It is an opportunity to become stronger. Nevertheless, because information reaches the site before magazines have been printed and distributed in certain parts of the world, it creates a risk that readers will rely on the Web and cut out the subscription. It will be well beyond 2010 before the revenue accruing to Web sites can match the revenue of the printed magazine.

There are magazines that exist only in an electronic format. The Microsoft organisation has set up *Slate*, a well regarded US site that attempts to be the *Newsweek* of the Web. It toyed with the idea of restricting the site to subscribers, then opened it to all and has more recently announced a return to subscriptions. *Slate* has not exploited the new medium to any great extent. The best indication that it is aware that the Internet has greater potential is with sections that allow readers to add chapters to a story that has been started by a published author.

Salon is equally highly regarded as the first true magazine in cyberspace. The site refreshes frequently and provides a wealth of archival material. There's an on going saga, and sections dedicated to areas of interest – the media for example. It is a clean site, with few images to slow access. The publishers are clearly aware of the limitations of the medium. Will *Slate* and *Salon* become the markers for the Internet magazines of the millennium? Probably not. If such exist, they are almost certainly in their infancy and little known at present. The content and presentation will vary according to the intended users. The presentation of magazines on the Internet has by no means reached its zenith. A new era for magazines is opening.

7 Newspapers

NEWSPAPERS have been redefining themselves ever since the advent of the radio. It will be remarkable if there were any let up to this process in the next ten years. Indeed it would be remarkable if the pressure on national, provincial and regional newspapers did not increase.

▲   ▲   ▲

As well as radio, newspapers have faced threats from first black and white and then colour tv. In each case the newspaper industry has responded. Now comes the threat from the Internet and the digital delivery of news direct to the receiver; 24 hours a day television news channels and Web sites which promise the classified advertiser a greater spread of possible purchasers than any single newspaper can deliver. Newspapers are under fire on all fronts.

But this is the way it will always be. Circulations across the world are in decline. A newspaper cannot survive on its heritage. It has continually to justify its own existence. However changes have been made. For instance no UK newspaper would now dare to appear without colour printing for both news pictures and advertising. The first efforts at colour news pictures by *Today* were derided as Eddieshahvision, and certainly the printing equipment chosen was not suitable for the purpose required. No colour newspaper now uses the configuration of press that

Today used initially. Newspapers and printing machine manufacturers have learned since those pioneering days. The current crop of presses offer high speed – almost 70,000 copies an hour today and 100,000 an hour shortly, and colour almost anywhere on the paper. The speed with which it is possible to replate for a new edition is faster than ever before and a range of options is promising to bring digital printing to presses in the foreseeable future. On the fly, plate change is being introduced on the newer generation of printing presses, machines that will last for the next 15 years. Moving from one edition to the next can be done without stopping the press and wasting just a dozen copies.

The leading newspaper press manufacturer, Goss Graphic Systems, has revealed its hand for a press for the next century. The inking system no longer relies on mixing an oil based ink with a largely water based fountain solution, through a chain of rollers and so to the printing plate. This has remained largely unchanged for a century and slows the starting up process. The Goss innovation is similar to the fuel injection systems that have replaced carburettors on petrol engines. Its digital inking system blends the ink and water in a mixer and injects this into the plate. It is fast and in tests has produced better quality than conventional inking systems. This remains a development project but is one that, once it proves successful as Goss is confident it will, will have a big impact on making newspapers easier to print. It will also improve the ability of one printing machine to match exactly the printing qualities of another press. This is a crucial requirement at a time when it is becoming easier to distribute a newspaper digitally and to print close to where the customers are. This trend is one that will need more satellite printing operations, often printing apparently rival newspapers at a time when advertisers and readers are less forgiving of poor quality colour printing.

It was once thought enough for a newspaper to print in colour. Now readers and advertisers expect newspaper colour to match that of other printing. The only way to come close to this ideal is through digital process control, where all the parameters on a printing press which might cause it to fluctuate are brought under digital control.

Other developments are introducing digitally controlled motors in place of mechanical gear drives and clutches. Again the advantage is that colour accuracy can be improved through control of the mechanical parts of a machine and start up is faster. It becomes easier to print shorter run papers, or papers with more frequent edition changes.

The Goss research and development team also envisages replacing the conventional flat aluminium printing plate with a printing cylinder which is slipped into place using air pressure. Gone are the spanners of old, reliant on the skill of the printer to position the plate accurately. The Goss cylinder system promises to be faster to change than plates.

The most intriguing of Goss's developments is the cylinder itself. This has a special coating which can be imaged by a laser to alter the electrical conductivity of the surface material. The whole cylinder, with an image area differently charged to the rest of the cylinder, is dipped into a bath of a copper solution. The image area becomes in effect copper plated and will then attract the ink necessary to make a printed image.

Even if Goss cannot make its technology commercially viable, it has opened the door to a number of other developers. MAN Roland has shown a laser imaged press where the cylinders are dipped in a bath of a wax-like substance. It dries on the cylinder and a laser can etch an image into the surface to carry ink to the paper. This is a gravure-like process, and again may never see the light of day as a commercial product. However by the end of the first decade of the next century it is certain that at least one digital printing technology will be in daily use by newspapers, if only in conjunction with their conventional presses. There will be a long transition period, as it will be too expensive in capital terms to move from an established technology to a less established technology. Newspaper publishers cannot afford interruptions to production because of developing technology.

Some newspapers are now using digital printing, making use of inkjet heads to add lucky numbers to the top or bottom of the paper. Each number is different and, even at 70,000 copies an hour, legible. The same technology will be used to add a late breaking story, replacing the Stop Press box which used to be a feature of letterpress printing. It has been impossible with offset printing to replicate the Stop Press, where a small story could be slotted onto the printing cylinder after the rest of the page was mounted and printing had begun. Stopping the press, adding the few extra lines of lead and starting again, was a matter of minutes. In offset litho where the entire plate has to be exposed, processed and then fitted to the press, Stop Press has become a thing of the past. A limited digital capability will restore this feature. The same technology might also be used to print a marketing message, perhaps providing local information to an otherwise global ad – the name and address of a local car dealer for instance.

DATA BASES

The barrier to precision targeting of newspapers is that newspaper publishers tend to know very little about their readers and certainly do not know their names and addresses. This is not the case throughout the world, and the database of readers or subscribers is going to become an essential tool in the next century. US publishers have been keen to gather demographic information, while many Scandinavian newspapers are distributed to subscribers via the postal system. In the UK, Associated Newspapers has considered recruiting its own network of home delivery staff to overcome the difficulties of obtaining information about its readers.

Newspapers already operate with databases, but are only now beginning to recognise the fact. The 21st century newspaper, whether publishing on paper or electronically, will be driven by its database.

This will manage all editorial matter, all pictures and graphics, the incoming advertisements, classified ads and will enable the most efficient distribution of all elements within a newspaper.

Newspapers have been buying computer systems to operate in different areas – Atex or SII front end systems for editorial, with sub systems to handle images. Even the newer installations are built around this model using standard platform computers, Macs or PCs instead of dedicated terminals. Each computer has a specific function, either editing, story creation or page make up with the required software loaded into that computer. Communication with other departments and archives is limited and difficult. Few newspapers have electronic archives of their material, something that will inevitably change as the need to reorganise material for electronic publication is realised.

Newspaper computer networks will move in two directions, not necessarily mutually exclusive. One direction will lead towards database-based publications, where all the electronic sources are held in one or more interconnected databases. As soon as information about news creation, ad booking and space allocation becomes dynamic, the digital newspaper is born. Many of the decisions that are taken well ahead of publication – the size of the paper, the amount to be filled by editorial, where the colour sections will fall and so on, will be left until the last moment. And this information will be conveyed direct to the printing operation which will put aside the correct number of paper reels and organise the press configuration to allow for the folder and colour printing units to be in the correct sequence.

For publishers, this provides more tools for the advertising department and more creative opportunities for the journalistic side. Costs are reduced, as many of the tasks that have been time consuming and manual will be automated. Dynamic systems such as this might yet produce the plethora of newspaper titles that was expected after the Wapping dispute broke the power of the printing unions in the UK.

NETWORKS

The second direction in which newspapers will move will free up the workstations from the dedicated tasks they currently perform. Newspapers will build intranets to connect all departments involved in the publishing process. These will allow a common browser to allow journalists, sub editors, designers, sales and administrative staff and editors, to access the software tools that are needed in their jobs. The software will be stored in a central file server and called down as needed. The required application will be called as a Java application. Of course Java may not be the operating system in a decade's time, and even if it is, it will have evolved tremendously to offer more complex and intriguing possibilities. However a distributed operating system language, independent of computer platform and its underlying operating system, and able to carry a range of applications, is going to become accepted.

The implications of dynamic newspaper networks, where staff can move from one place to another without losing access to their files, is going to be profound. The traditional newsroom is under threat, and with it the cameraderie that journalists have grown up with. With distributed systems, journalists can be in different rooms, different locations, even different countries and still be on the story.

The School of Mass Communications at Virginia Commonwealth University in Richmond, Virginia in the USA, has set up a prototype 21st century newsroom. This envisages a sound-controlled open concept newsroom, where seating and meeting areas are flexible to allow for as free a flow of information and people as possible. Large flat panel displays will show the state of the story in progress, pages being put together on the event schedules that the newspaper is covering.

The network infrastructure envisaged is based on infrared wireless connections, though a cable network with nodes that individuals can plug into would serve just as well. Each of the workstations will give journalists access to wire services, video feeds and the Internet, as well as the publisher's internal resources. The video capability will be used for conferencing purposes, with journalists and others unable to be present physically.

The paper's archive will be crucial. Virginia calls this a Cybery, pooling information from across the world and also tracking how each story is being put together, the staff allocated to it and progress. It expects this Planning Assignment Coordination and Quality system to be a central function of the newspaper. The project is dependent on using applications that exist already, but nevertheless points the way towards a newsroom where producing stories for publication in a printed format is not the first requirement.

The finished story, if any report in a dynamic environment can be considered finished, will be published in a variety of media, including on-line and Internet. This medium has, from the outset, had a strong emphasis on feedback, the right to instant reply and opinion. This aspect will be strengthened in future and journalists must expect some instant reaction from readers.

CLASSIFIED

The classified advertising department has been the most advanced in terms of database usage. A caller can be sold into multiple or selected editions of a paper, for different time periods, with different appearances and be billed accordingly.

It is a section of the newspaper that is under most threat from the new generation of publishers. By the early part of the next century, Microsoft's initial incarnation as a software developer will have given way to a primary function as a publisher. The ownership of content and copyright is driving Bill Gates to assemble massive picture libraries and to publish them digitally. Convergence is not restricted to Microsoft. Time Warner has bought Turner Broadcasting, NBC has a partnership with Microsoft.

The Internet channels are the result, with the Microsoft Network's Sidewalk and America Online's Digital Cities, leading the way. These ventures are publishing listings that have been a staple of provincial newspapers. The next steps are accommodation for sale and rent, cars and personal sales. By 2001, US consultancy group Forrester Research reckons that newspapers risk the loss of 10 per cent of their revenues to on-line classified advertising.

Newspaper publishers for their part have moved classified operations on-line and it may be that their experience will win out. However the size of communities that the much larger operators like Microsoft, or search engine providers like Yahoo and Infoseek can address, gives them an advantage. There is much to be said, however, for retaining a strong local connection and other newspapers, both in the UK and the USA will meet the challenge halfway and pool resources to build extensive networks that allow users to be as specific or as wide ranging as they would like.

The key to establishing a successful classified ad service electronically is the intuitiveness and ease of use of the search engine. Those that can devise a search engine that is simultaneously comprehensive, simple to use and able to cope with user mistakes, will be the winner. Some form of intelligent software, that learns from key words used what items are being sought, is needed. Other publishers will offer push technologies, allowing a user to enter a job specification or description of an ideal house or car, and the software will automatically match these requirements against the incoming ads. If there's a match, the user will receive an e-mail or a copy of the ad sent direct to the desktop.

The printing plants are already sophisticated enough to divide a print run by its destination, usually the warehouse outside a large town. Providing shrink wrapped or strapped bundles for delivery to individual newsagents is already possible. Newspapers, particularly regional dailies, have started to exploit this by ensuring that the bundles destined for newsagents in the suburbs are those that receive the gardening supplements. Those with inner city addresses receive the city night life magazines.

It can go further and it will. Robert Maxwell began a crude attempt to gather lifestyle and other information about readers in a *Daily Mirror* Club. Like the supermarket loyalty card, the club member received additional benefits over the non-member reading the newspaper. In exchange, the publisher built up a database of valuable, marketable information about his readers. The *Mirror*'s attempt did not last long, but in any case it was then too early to see any real benefit from the data that might have been gathered.

Clearly, if a reader's likes and dislikes are known and a publisher can provide this sort of information to his advertisers and create almost customised newspapers for the readers, then he has a very powerful marketing tool. It was this that provided the impetus for the explosion of free newspapers in the 1980s. 30 years on however, it will be the ability to customise that makes the difference. A local newspaper in North London might produce editions featuring Arsenal on one back page and Tottenham on another. In Manchester different editions might favour United or City.

PRINTING

The printing technology that dominates will continue to be web offset litho, mainly because of the huge tonnages of metal already in place. However digital printing will become extremely important, particularly in producing hybrid publications where the numbers for a customised print run fall below economic levels. Technological development will help bring this break point lower. Plate making will be faster and more accurate and it will be easier to prepare presses for printing, and far easier to match one printing machine with another, whether alongside the first or in a different part of the country.

Remote or satellite printing becomes increasingly important to cut lead times and reduce road travel. Complete digital editions of a newspaper will be sent to plants closer to where the readers are. This is only sensible if levels of quality can be maintained over huge distances. Associated Newspapers, publisher of the *Daily Mail,* has led the way in developing a colour matching system that operates across the printing sites it uses, from Bristol to Southampton to London, the midlands and the north east. The software ensures that the variations in the printing characteristics of each printing press – its fingerprint – are provided for, by adjusting the file as it arrives from the head office. The result is that the paper will look the same, regardless of where it has been printed.

The next stage, and one that has not been implemented yet, is to have the image the press can generate dictate the previous preparatory steps. This is unlike the situation where film and a proof are created to match the advertiser's wishes only to result in disappointment when the finished page does not match. In future, the image will be generated on a monitor on the press and this, rather than a proof, will be used to judge the incoming ad. It is a lengthy process that demands expertise and is expensive.

In the hybrid world, the ability to print on multiple sites will still not be enough to target the paper precisely. The Massachusetts Institute of Technology has been involved in many projects under the banner of News in the Future. One that has been tested provides a section of a newspaper printed on a shop's premises, which is slipped into the paper that is sold over the counter. In the MIT experiment, the hybrid paper was targeted at an immigrant Asian population concentrated in one locality. The digitally produced section carried news from Gujerat, the home region of many of the potential readers. The City's newspaper would not have carried what was essentially very parochial news for a small section of its readership, interested in the results of sports events, births, marriages and deaths so far from the USA. Yet by providing the supplement, a specific section of the readership has been served.

A similar concept lay behind a project that Scitex launched under the name Pointcast. Its idea was that leading hotels around the world would install an inkjet printer, sold by Scitex and use this to print copies of newspapers for their business guests. A handful of hotels agreed to pilot the project, as did a sample of newspaper publishers. However the equipment proved unreliable, the cost per copy too expensive, and the alternatives – having a flown-in copy or using television to keep up to date with the news – combined to thwart the product.

This idea may well revive, since some of the barriers to its development are being removed. The inkjet printing equipment, whether from Scitex or elsewhere, is more reliable and considerably more cost effective, speeds of data transfer are improving and the file sizes are being kept lower. Furthermore, the entire industry is adopting as a standard format the compact portable document format produced by Adobe. The technical barriers may be coming down, but cultural barriers may prove harder to shift.

THE 'DAILY ME'

Two other factors combine to reduce the chances of this product succeeding. One is the world newspaper, the other the *Daily Me*. The world newspaper is printed at numerous locations outside the traditional base. The *International Herald Tribune* has long led the way as the international paper for US nationals abroad. However it is in many ways a conservative product. As such it has been overtaken by the *Wall Street Journal* moving east across the Atlantic and by the *Financial Times* moving in the opposite direction. Like many of their readers, these newspapers have become multinationals. Others will follow suit. For Associated, having set up the network of remote sites in the UK, it will not be difficult to add a printing operation close to an expatriate community, in Tokyo say, or Los Angeles. There is little to stop this happening now.

A greater threat in the future is the Internet. An immediate perception of the World Wide Web was that it sounded the death knell for newspapers, because everybody would want their news faster than a paper product could provide it and they would want only the stories that they wished to read. Nicholas Negroponte, the US academic who has evangelised about the possibilities of the Internet, has dubbed this the *Daily Me*.

The *Daily Me* – (like the *Daily Leyland* in Chapter 1) is a compilation of the news stories gathered from around the globe and filtered, so that what is presented is matched to an individual's tastes. The *Daily Me* can be viewed on screen, with hyperlinks to video reports or to further text, adding to the experience. It can also be downloaded to a Web page and automatically printed each morning, timed to coincide with the alarm going off, to be read with a slice of toast and cup of coffee.

Because I have provided the information by which to filter the news that I am interested in, I have built up a profile that is of enormous use to an advertiser. Before long, advertisers will be demanding to see such demographic information from Web sites.

The technical problems associated with production of an aesthetically pleasing *Daily Me* are a long way from being solved. In the meantime, the first applications that can provide some of the tools needed for Web-based newspaper publication are emerging. Pointcast will deliver news stories as they happen, on a ticker tape that scrolls across the base of a computer screen. However the system has a vast capacity for data streams, so it will either have to wait for data capacity to be increased, or for a more compact version to become available.

It works by continually trawling the Web for stories, which either match the company names which the user has selected, or else relate to chosen subject areas. These are then presented as breaking news. The drawbacks are that it only becomes news when a release hits the Web, and also that the news release is more often than not a press statement rather than a written, edited and submitted report from a qualified journalist. There is no judgement attached to the story, which is where Pointcast in its present state will fail.

There are other news channels available on the Web. First off are the news areas on a number of search engines. These can be tailored to match a user's profile and are a means to increase traffic to the Web site. Again, there is as yet no attempt to add any journalistic content to the stories, other than that provided by the news organisations such as Reuters. Things will improve when some of the larger news organisations sign up to provide the news analysis and feed that these Internet services require.

The news organisations however, believe that their own Web sites can be attractive enough to survive as electronic equivalents to the newsprint product which begat them. The *Electronic Telegraph*, spawn of the *Daily Telegraph*, was the first in the UK to enter the fray. It provides the news, the sport and the analysis that the paper provides, with extensive linking to other sources of information. If Negroponte is right, and people want customised information in swiftly digestible bites, then the *Electronic Telegraph* is the equivalent of a long lunch at the buffet table.

In editorial terms it is rated a success. In commercial terms it remains a fledgling compared to the traditional title. So it is with other publishers, whether adopting the *Telegraph* pattern or opting, as the *Guardian* is doing, for something almost completely different. Its editor Ian Katz has admitted he is playing the long game and is aiming to build an on-line community. This will have a greater chance of success than replicating the newspaper, particularly as few conventional editors are going to want to see the electronic offspring break a story before the paper itself. Until newspaper Web sites are free to scoop the paper, they will be vulnerable to other, less restricted news providers.

ADVERTISING

Another problem that traditional news publishers face is the drive to raise revenue. The advertising model is not developed and while this is sure to have matured over the next 10 years, this is a long time to fund an expensive development. Attempts at charging a subscription have failed, causing a massive drop off in visits and a rapid rethink of the subscription policy. Only in areas where the newspaper is virtually a business tool, have subscriptions had any success. This will remain the case. Unless the user is receiving privileged information, difficult to obtain elsewhere, levying a subscription will not be a model for success.

Equally at threat is the classified revenue that local and regional newspapers have come to regard as their own. The attractions of advertising to untold millions on the Web, rather than a few tens of thousands in a single edition of a newspaper, are obvious. The race to develop the perfect Internet classified ad package is on.

However attempts in the UK to develop recruitment advertising over the Web have so far failed, due to the problems of training job seekers to access their Web browser. Likewise there is little point is attempting to sell an item of everyday furniture over the Web if the responses are going to come from buyers too remote to be of any practical use. The local newspaper will retain a vital role.

When it comes to selling more expensive items, where the buyers are more limited, then the Web will come into its own to the detriment of newspapers. Certain cars and houses will be sold in greater volume electronically then through the newspaper. Likewise, listings information will work as well in an electronic format as on the page. Newspaper publishers are going to have to come to terms with these developments, either by deciding to stand aside or by joining in. The local newspaper networks in the UK and elsewhere provide the basis for some cooperative effort. The local newspaper has the tremendous advantage of knowing both its advertisers and its readers. It also has the database created to produce the newsprint version, but which can equally operate in the on-line world. The local newspaper also has the established name in its community as the provider of such information.

Expect newspapers to snap up Internet classified advertising providers as they emerge from being anything more than a flea bite irritation. However conventional publishers may not be able to do this with the new breed of content providers. These new news organisations will be split, from the single man operation providing an electronic e-mail service, through to the Microsoft Network style operations, aiming, like Disney, to create an all-encompassing environment that the dedicated customer never has to leave. Both Davids and Goliaths will be amongst the future news providers. But the newspaper publishers will come to realise that their key asset is information, and the key requirement dissemination of that information as quickly and accurately as possible. It will mean that the *Daily Me* will be *My Version of the Daily Tribune*, and that the artficial restriction of waiting until press time to distribute a story will be removed.

Just as newspapers adjusted to accommodate radio and television, so they will evolve in the next century. They will be conscious that their readers, to a greater or lesser degree (depending on the demographics of their constituency) will be getting information via screens. The movement for newspapers to explain and entertain will continue, as will the need for them to justify themselves through investigation and analysis of the news.

The newspaper itself will be in colour throughout. It may well have a slip-in, digitally printed local section, or a section for a reader's particular community. Each report will have a Web address for further information on the same subject, or perhaps a reminder to check an e-mail account.

8 The New Book

WHILE he printed book has held sway for 500 years, there is no guarantee that this will remain the case into the new millennium. Already CD-Roms are forcing directory publications onto the defensive; just around the corner is the concept of the electronic book, perhaps using a CD, perhaps not; the hybrid publication, using the resources of CD and Internet combined, threatens the established order in some professional markets. In short, for many publications in the next century, the printed and bound book or magazine will be an option rather than the natural choice.

▲ ▲ ▲

The impact has been greatest in reference publishing where printed volumes are now rarer than electronic versions. Nowhere is this clearer than with the *Encyclopaedia Britannica*, which after several years of persistence with its bound version, has now announced that the CD version will be the most important. This is partly down to cost. The bound versions are around £3,000 a set while the CD, though less aesthetically pleasing, retails for little more than £100. It is partly down to competition, where rival reference tomes have become accepted as the standard, squeezing out *Britannica*. The most important of these is Microsoft's *Encarta*, a version of which is given away with almost every PC destined for home use. And most importantly for *Britannica*, a good proportion of those buying *Encarta* will upgrade to the following year's version. An encyclopaedia is no longer a once in a life time purchase, but a regular investment.

The third influence is down to the technology. *Britannica* has been available on the five inch platter before, but only with the most recent edition has the publisher begun to explore the possibilities offered by sound and motion. These possibilities are somewhat restricted with the conventional CD, but the forthcoming Digital Versatile Disc (DVD) , a disc which retains the familiar format but has boosted memory capacity around eight times. The potential for inserting motion and sound, interactivity, search engines and so forth are limited only by the skills and imagination of the production teams. The paper publication doesn't stand a chance.

However compelling content is not enough. Companies like Dorling & Kindersley, which have plunged into multi-media publishing, have found the water a little chillier than they anticipated. At the end of 1997, the company halved the workforce dedicated to CD-Rom development in order to save £3m and return the division to profit. The problem is that consumers have tended to equate the price of the multi-media with the price of the printed version. Then there is the little matter of the limited audience, for while a majority of the population has reading skills, only a relatively small percentage has a suitable computer at home. Even by 2000, it is estimated that only 40 per cent of UK households will have a computer at home, not all of these with CD drives. The market certainly has potential, but it has so far failed to live up to it.

Provided the high levels of investment continue, a greater range of electronic product is going to appear and the improvement in the level of authoring software will reduce the costs associated with CD development. These are put as high as £300,000 a title, raising the end price to the consumer and deterring a number of publishers from a full scale commitment to the market. As the initial investment required falls and the market develops, other publishers will return. For the moment this has meant that many of the titles available in the UK have come from the USA where the market is potentially that much greater, so content has had a North American skew.

Prices have fallen tremendously. The first CD editions of *Compton's New Media* sold for $895 in 1991 but fell to $150 by 1996. Average UK prices have dropped from around £50 to less than £20. The greatest misunderstanding however, has been that publishers have considered multi-media publication as an extension of book publishing and not an extension of the computer industry.

Far more product is sold through the likes of PC World than WH Smith. The initial problems, associated with a tendency to throw conventional titles at an electronic format without consideration for that format, will disappear with experience. There needs to be far more structure to electronic reference material than an alphabetical listing and index at the back.

The demand for multi-media publications will grow when the prices drop to the near equivalent of the paper publication. Work is needed too on the structure of the content and the user interface needed to come to grips with the CD format. As the current generation of school children, familiar with the CD from their education, leaves school, they will bring with them the intuitive knowledge of how to work the technology – something their parents don't have. It is to be hoped that those managing CD development projects gain a greater understanding of the medium, since much of what has been accepted into the home is the result of design by geeks for geeks.

The importance of the education market to the CD publisher is underlined by the increased emphasis on this section of the market by Dorling & Kindersley. The company reckons that two thirds of the 20-30 titles it generates each year will be aimed at children, compared to 20 per cent previously. Self-help leisure products will also have a great future in a multi-media format. An instructional golf title would score over the printed guide by including video clippings. It would score over the video by being quicker to access and by giving control to the user. Future technology will allow golfers to feed their own video footage into the computer to overlay their swing against that being demonstrated. Further software would then give the appearance of analysing the errors. What holds for golf is equally effective in fishing, cookery or gardening, – any publication that now sells significant volumes on video.

HYBRID PRODUCTS

However the greatest opportunity open to multi-media products is the emergence of the DVD as a replacement for the CD. This will made hybrid video and print products far richer, though whether these will continue to be produced by existing paper publishers is open to doubt. Far more likely is that there will be a number of joint ventures between organisations keen to exploit the new medium, but lacking the skill set to do so effectively. While DVD appears to answer many prayers, its introduction is beset by the sort of uncertainties associated with the introduction of the first video cassette recorders – namely which format will become the standard. At its most basic, a DVD will hold 4.7Gb of information on a single sided disk. Specifications exist for a version which is double sided and has a dual information carrying layer, taking capacity to 17Gb.

Despite the slow take off of multi-media publishing, a vast number of companies is keen to be involved. In 1992 the *Multimedia Yearbook* found 698 companies producing 487 titles. In 1997 this had grown to 9,147 companies and 13,000 products. Not all these will be publishers. In revenue terms the market for business multi-media publications is expected to grow from $453m in 2000 across Europe, to $2,077m five years later. The biggest growth will be in on-line services, but CD-based material will grow 300 per cent in that period. In the consumer sector, the European market was worth £120m in 1994 and the UK alone is expected to achieve a $1 billion market by 2005.

The death of the CD has been as widely predicted as that of its emergence to take over from print. The information it contains is supposed to migrate to the Internet, where data can be updated instantly and need never go out of date. However the CD will retain its position. Working on-line will remain frustratingly slow. To some extent, it will remain an uncontrollable cost and with connection charges and subscription charges may well work out more expensive than a CD. A CD is also tangible, portable evidence of ownership.

The data is accessible far more quickly and it is a far more reliable method of obtaining information than the sometimes quixotic Internet. What will emerge instead is a range of hybrid products, combining the best of the CD for accessing large amounts of data quickly and of the Internet for providing up to the minute information. This makes the hybrid product more valuable in a professional or business environment than a consumer area, although a product selling second hand cars linked to a web site containing an updated list of prices would have considerable consumer appeal.

One of the first hybrid programs to be launched was IVY Binder, a spin-off from the Word Perfect company. The application had been developed for in-house use, keeping developers up to date with the latest announcements. The company has been pitching at magazine publishers wanting to make their products available in electronic formats. Material is held as pdf files, retaining the appearance of the printed page. The level of functionality is decided by the publisher, but can include searchable archives of previous material. A refinement is that where a story changes – a piece on computer technology for instance – the IVY Binder software will over-write with the up to date information. This is where the power of the hybrid product comes in. The original may be stored on the CD, but the update is provided across the Internet at the discretion of the publisher. The publisher earns a subscription income which is essential, since without it, half the advantage of the product is taken away. To the end user, where the information is, whether held locally on a CD, whether under a master licence on the local area network, or whether in the central remote database, is irrelevant and invisible. The publisher and application provide the context for the documents.

Similar archive management software is available as MediaSphere from Cascade Systems. It too uses pdf documents and a powerful natural language search engine to locate and retrieve articles held on a database. The product has so far been aimed at magazine publishers for their own electronic archive, though it is possible to allow access across the Internet. The CD is not the only competition to the established order. The long awaited electronic book is about to make an appearance, with its backers vociferous in their claims for the technology. However neither the Everybook nor the Softbook have yet reached the public, though both have been shown at exhibitions, sometimes working, sometimes not. The concept is a lightweight, compact, computer display that opens like a book to reveal two opposing screens like an open book. The first version of the Everybook is a leather encased volume which turns on when open and off when closed. The opening screen is a collection of thumbnail images of all the material stored, arranged to suit the reader. The reader selects by touching the screen, there being no mouse or keyboard to work through. Finger pressure is used to turn pages and navigation – for example returning to the main screen.

EVERYBOOK

Everybook is the brainchild of Daniel Munyan, now president of Everybook Inc. The concept has been developed since 1995 with the introduction of the first Everybook Readers due this year. Munyan argues that the concept of the paperless office failed, because computer operators tend to print out what is on screen, edit on paper, then input the corrections. The apocryphal story is that the idea came to the inventor when, on a long flight, a fellow passenger was struggling to read by the overhead light. By the end of the flight the concept and business plan had been written down. Everybook was on its way. Its progress has been somewhat erratic, dogged by problems of reducing the weight and increasing the battery power. Neither problem is a long term difficulty and will be resolved before 2010. The chosen processor comes from specialist firm Advanced Micro Devices, since its processors are less power hungry than most.

The initial concept is to put Everybook Readers in the hands of professionals and students. The students have been the first market – initial work being done with educational publishers who were approached about making their material available. The texts will be held as pdf in a series of Everybook Stores – Virtual shops on the Internet that allow the user to browse, select and download the selected title. The browsing process is in colour, allowing presentation of cover designs. Munyan explains: "Once you're on-line with us, when you touch the Everybook Store icon on the screen, you will see a full colour virtual bookstore. To browse, you touch a subject shelf, making it come forward so you can see the books on it. Touch the cover thumbnail of a publication and the cover will fill the screen. Touch it again and you have the contents page. A book will take two to three minutes to download and the Reader will hold hundreds of books in read-only format."

The text can be printed out, but in order to preserve copyright, a large watermark is automatically added in an attempt to defeat fraud. Munyan argues that publishers will support his venture as it offers a respectable way of moving into electronic distribution without the risk associated with unlicensed publication on the Internet, which will provide no income for publisher and author. The first books will be academic or technical books, where the page costs are high and the audience limited. The second area is for professionals in healthcare, the law and engineering, where there are frequent changes to essential information – a market that IVY Binder had noted. These users will also be prepared to pay for a device that provides the rapid updates relevant to their professional lives. The other advantages that Everybook provides will be used to underline the consumer launch of the product, scheduled for 2000, but which is almost certain to be delayed to an unknown extent. These include the original inspiration – the possibility of reading in bed or on a flight without disturbing your partner or neighbour. Secondly the device will play an environmental card, explaining that publication via the screen will be good for the environment, since no trees are destroyed to create the publication.

In a statement to tie in with the first announcement of the Everybook, Munyan explained that "the concept would have a positive effect on the environment due to the fact that paper and pulp manufacture and book/magazine printing are among the top 20 worst polluting industries. Low grade paper disposal is also a serious burden on the environment. Everybook eliminates paper and ink from publishing, while preserving the beauty and functionality of the printed word." It will also preserve what will be a closed network. The Everybook format, while based around the *de facto* standard of pdf also has distinguishing features that ensure that it is a proprietary environment. This means that there is a risk that a rival electronic book may gain a larger market share early on, and whatever the merits of the technology, become the dominant force. At the heart is the technology used and its reliability. The system has to be robust, yet light, powerful but not power consuming and above all priced correctly. Even then Everybook may not win. There will even be desk versions, perhaps built into a desk.

Other readers will become available, perhaps based on portable computer technology, perhaps not. Associated Newspapers' technical director Allan Marshall, has long considered an electronic book that is carried in a brief case a suitable device for reading the latest edition of a newspaper downloaded by wireless communications. In the USA, Knight-Ridder has been investigating a light electronic reading tablet. At the other end of the scale, the *Leicester Mercury* experimented with a series of display boards that could be positioned in shopping centres and show the latest front page. In this instance, the newspaper page would be transmitted to the electronic display, where a low cost laser would charge a moveable belt. As this passed through a bath of toner particles, they would be picked up by the charged areas and so form a large format poster for the newspaper.

The Everybook Store is not the only repository of electronic books on the Internet. Publishers and book stores may make books or parts of books available on the Net, with these intended to promote the sale of paper based products however produced. Others are listing complete texts of out of copyright titles. These are available to down-load and print at home on a laser printer. The Teleread campaign in the USA is seeking to use electronic publications as a means of increasing the nation's literacy rates. The user would be able to read any book for free, while the national government would fund the royalty payments to publishers and authors according to their popularity.

The campaign is lobbying for widespread distribution of computers to read the material and has priced the cost of creating the TR[Teleread]Net. However it is most unlikely to have a major impact on the publishing industry which favours conventional means of payment in exchange for a physical product.

THE NOVEL

The digital revolution not only opens new ways of creating books, but also new possibilities for books themselves. This may include the 'future of the novel' experiments in form and content, redefining how a book should be. There have been a number of hypertext novels, using the ability of the electronic medium to leap around according to links set in the text. The narrative structure associated with the novel is destroyed in favour of something akin to a game. To those used to being led by the author, the experience of a hypertext book is bewildering, infuriating even. It is doubtful that the definitive hypertext novel has yet been written, making the form something of a curiosity and perhaps an experimental dead end. However the generation that has grown up accustomed to sound bite information, the MTV culture and a flood of different information sources and is perfectly comfortable reading from a screen, may be more open to the hypertext book. There are software applications available to help construct the parts of a story, from the various points of view or angles that the author wishes to include. For most readers, the hypertext work will be too demanding compared to starting at the beginning of a book and working through, chapter by chapter, until the end.

Not so far removed from the hypertext novel are certain computer games. The *Myst* and *Riven* titles are engaging and avoid the 'shoot 'em up' approach while unfolding a story with which the game player becomes involved. Douglas Adams, author of the *Hitchhiker's Guide to the Galaxy* series, is taking a not dissimilar approach through a computer game he has authored called *Starship Titanic*. Somewhere between the post modernist approach of the hypertext novel and the computer game, lies a new genre of entertainment.

There are other less revolutionary approaches to the electronic novel, exploiting some of the features of the digital age. Amazon.com, the Internet book store, commissioned John Updike to pen the first paragraph of a mystery novel which was then published on the web site. Visitors to the site were then invited to submit paragraphs to add to the initial text. An editorial team selected the best and added these to the continuing saga. After 44 submissions, John Updike added a final paragraph to complete a new John Updike novel billed as his first murder mystery story. A different approach on the Microsoft Network had visitors voting on how the story was to progress, selecting from paragraphs written by published authors. Its first experiment produced something of curiosity rather than literary merit. However such collaborative novels are likely to increase. If nothing else, digital communications make it easy to send chapters to a partner across the globe instantly.

9 Printing

HAD William Caxton been able to visit a book printer in the mid 1960s he would have recognised the printing techniques in use. The letterpress process then predominant, used metal type, ink rolled on to the type and contact between type and paper to create the image. This had hardly altered since the end of the fifteenth century. The printing factory would have been a clanking, hissing place, with printing machines big enough for a man to walk beneath, piles of partly printed work stored across the floor, dirty walls and windows almost impenetrable by daylight.

▲   ▲   ▲

50 years on, things look very different. Gone are the metal type and locked up chases. The large presses have been retired and the environment in the 21st century book printer is almost clinically clean. The printing devices are greyish boxes, accepting a reel of white paper in one end and delivering a printed reel at the other. A folder and trimmer delivers folded and cut sections ready for immediate binding. The binder is next to the press and has been set up automatically with parameters to suit the newly printed book.

The difference between the printer of only 35 years ago and the printer 15 years hence, is that in the future there will be no partly completed books, no stacks of printed sections awaiting folding and sewing. Instead the digital printing machines will print the entire title in one pass, each page in its correct place. There will be no lengthy set up, involving intricate adjustments by skilled machine minders. Instead an operator will press a button, probably in a separate room and quite possibly hundreds of miles or even a continent, away.

THE DOCUTECH

The revolution can be dated to 1991 and the introduction of the Docutech, the Xerox high speed laser printer. This works with sheeted paper and prints by an electrophotographic process. Instead of transferring an image to a copying drum through an arrangement of lens and lamps, a laser is used to write the image directly on the drum. The master imaging technique, in which rapid scan lines are used to build up the image, is common to all digital imagesetters where lasers are able to operate accurately at up to 4,000 dots per inch.

Xerox was happy with 600dpi, which is coming close to printing industry quality, once reckoned to have 1,000dpi as a quality threshold. Xerox had easily improved on the IBM supported digital printing standard of 240dpi, and with printing speeds of more than 100 pages a minute, volume digital printing had arrived. Further improvements were necessary, including the ability to accept PostScript files, before the Docutech could build as strong a position in the printing industry as its copiers had built up in the office sector. The Docutech itself was never conceived as a dedicated book printing machine. Because it works from relatively small sheets, the finishing stages would be too complex and clumsy for dedicated book production. This did not prevent many printers using Docutechs as the only available technology for the task, and it did not stop Docutechs being used to produce thousands of reports and short run directories, where the quality of the binding was secondary to the information contained. However the print-on-demand aspect, where a complete book could be printed in sequence, with no make ready time, was the real breakthrough.

By the mid 1990s, many book printers had Docutechs in place to handle work where this sort of turnaround and short print runs were necessary and the slightly different quality was acceptable. City printing, where reports have to be produced overnight with low print runs, was dominated by the technology.

Surrey book printer, Biddles, considered a print run of 250 copies to be the absolute minimum before adding Docutechs to its line up of conventional printing presses. Now a single copy is justifiable. Managing director Mick Read explains how this has helped publishers. "Digital printing takes the risk out of publishing and speeds up cash flow. We have produced a highly specialised book for one of our customers, whose potential total sales barely stretched to 100. Conventional printing, with a realistic minimum of 250, would have left him with at least 150 copies unsold."

LASER PRINTERS

However two further developments were needed before digital printing could become the most important book production technology. First was a new Adobe Rip, developed as the Supra, but quickly marketed under the name Extreme. Instead of handling PostScript, with its unpredictable file sizes, this was developed to use the portable document format, a compact page description language with very much smaller file sizes than PostScript. As a result, the ripping speeds were much faster than PostScript (see Chapter 5). Secondly the Extreme Rip could be mounted in pairs or more, and thus was able to drive the new generation of high speed laser printers at their full speed. Further production enhancements were the result of more powerful computer processors.

The new generation of laser printers introduced web printing, albeit on relatively narrow webs, but with a far higher productivity than before.

IBM Printing Systems adapted what had been a high speed systems printer used in data processing departments to print, not sprocket fed paper, but plain paper. Immediately, here was a digital printing machine that could be used for printing books at a decent rate and because the unit delivered folded sections, with print on both sides, its potential as a high speed book printing press was realised immediately. IBM sold Infoprint 4000s to almost all UK book printers, while those that did not buy from IBM invested in equivalent machines from Océ, which had bought Siemens Nixdorf, or one of a number of others.

Among the early adopters of the web fed digital printing technology was Butler & Tanner, placing the press in its Selwood Printing subsidiary. There, managing director Andrew Lowdon stressed: "Digital printing is an opportunity to lay the foundations for a radically different printing industry – one based on service rather than manufacturing. No longer will a customer have to produce more than is required. For monochrome work at least, print-on-demand has arrived." Selwood is the group's specialist short run printing operation, producing directory type books, but it is an indication that a company known as one of the leading book printers in the UK is prepared to start thinking in digital terms. Likewise great rival, Bath Press, went digital with the Infoprint 4000 almost in the same week. A seminar organised by Oscar Friedheim, the supplier of the specialist systems from Hunkeler, needed to fold and cut the printed web, pulled representatives from almost every UK book printer. The interest in digital printing would be turned into real investment in the following years.

Further work with IBM widened the types of paper that these printing machines could use. The nature of electrophotographic printing process puts a lot of stress on the paper, as the toner used to make the image is fused by heat after printing. Nevertheless an IBM customer in Chicago, printing books-on-demand, managed to print with what amounted almost to onion skin stocks. Printing speeds leapt ahead to reach a standard of more than 1,000pp a minute, (all potentially different) before the end of 1998. At this speed, the Infoprint 4000 was printing at an equivalent to a litho press running at 8,000 sheets an hour.

The laser printer has come under challenge from high speed ink jet printing. Scitex had a product capable of printing at 240dpi to suit the variable information requirements of data processing departments, but used mostly in direct mail printing. The ink jet head itself had a limited size, but mounting several together provided a page wide printing area. UK company Xaar was meanwhile working on a page wide printer, able to print 100pp a minute. The option was there to mount several of these together and increase the printing speed. The bonus to the Xaar system was that it printed in full colour and at high quality.

However, for all the advantages of digital printing, conventional litho printing and even some letterpress, will continue for books. When it comes to longer print runs, (anything above 1,000 copies) the conventional technology, albeit enormously enhanced, will remain. Digital controls on presses produce better quality printing and provide the ability to set them up faster and with fewer staff. One effect of this will be to split the book printing industry into those working with large sheets, or large format web presses, and those working with smaller format presses, able to turn work round faster than previously. Digital control of the pressroom links through to administration systems and to databases. These will hold libraries of books, duplicating those that the publishers have, but held in a printing format, namely pdf.

Imaging will be direct to plate, either an aluminium plate or a polyester material. The plate is loaded automatically into the press and fitted to the press almost instantly. The changeover time from one job to the next is a matter of minutes, making smaller format litho presses competitive in terms of productivity against both larger format machines and digital presses. Setting up the binders and casing machines is also a matter for digital control, again reducing time and increasing productivity.

To make this work, the printer has needed to invest in database technology, holding work in progress on file servers in the pdf page independent format. It becomes a straightforward task to direct these pages towards either the digital or the conventional printing route including the assembly of these pages into plates. The decision on how many to print and which system to use can be made late in the day. Apart from some special jobs which will be set up well in advance, printers will be expected to produce books overnight or at the very least within 24 hours. This makes sense when information can be fed from the publisher's computer system directly to the printer's. There may be triggers in place to keep the number of books in the shops at a constant level. Data from the high street Epos systems will feed to the publishers and on to the printers. A similar system already operates for Compact Disks where printers and pressing lines are tied to the sales systems managed by the music companies.

At short run book specialist Anthony Rowe, the company batches such orders in groups of 10. However while the printer is already set up, its sales director Ian Hilder points out that the publishers are lagging. "They have to sort themselves out in terms of being able to handle a low volume of orders." As a printer, the company's experience is representative of what others will find in the future. It already works with almost 500 live customers and handles thousands of orders each year. This places a heavy burden on the company's internal systems, especially as it is earning a reputation for handling work for small publishers, including a burgeoning number of almost vanity publishing titles. "It's because we can produce small quantities to a good standard at an economic price. These customers want to produce a book but don't see it as a commercial venture."

SELF-PUBLISHING

Would-be authors have a further option, thanks to the Internet. Sites exist offering the opportunity to have books printed exploiting the short run technology. One of the first is Xlibris, promising not even to charge the author for printing. Only the buyer pays. 'For that reason, the cost of publication on Xlibris is one-tenth the cost of publication anywhere else in the world today, allowing any author to publish, and any book to stay in print forever.' The company has some more conventional policies as well. The site contains an extensive database of professionally published titles. The buyer can order a book which Xlibris will print to order. Alternately the buyer can download an e-mail version of the text in pdf, and take on the responsibility for printing. This will become an increasingly common means of distribution, with implications for copyright and rights management.

The author subscribing to the Xlibris self-publish package is offered a number of modules. The author receives a home page on the Web site through which the books are listed. The company provides an editing environment, a set of virtual galley proofs to check and, once the author has decided the book is ready, he or she can decide to publish. There will be encouragement to buy author's copies, but effectively that is it. The final service is to monitor the number of people viewing the tome or buying it.

Another service offering to publish a book on-line is rather more blatant about its methods. 'eBooks Online is the easiest, most inexpensive way for authors to publish their book without having to find a literary agent or spend huge sums of money up front for printing!' The company, based in Malibu, California, produces a menu of charges starting with the basic price of $979 for a text of 150,000 words and 10 images. Additional images are charged at $10 a photo or line art original over and above the 10 that are included in the package price, and an extra fee of $100 per 1,000 words above the 150,000 word barrier.

Along with the text, eBook prints a 500 word biography and offers the opportunity to have a chapter from the book published in a free browse section of the Web site. The concept is that purchasers will come by, like what they see and download (at a small cost) a copy of a book that no conventional publisher would wish to put his name to. This is the beauty and the danger of self-publishing over the Internet. It is simple and direct, but there is no control, allowing distasteful as well as poorly written work the chance of a wider distribution.

PRINTER-PUBLISHER RELATIONSHIP

In the USA, digital printing is not confined to entrepreneurs and established printers. Ingram Books, the largest distributor of books in the United States, moved into print-on-demand, not to usurp the printer-publisher relationship, but to 'extend the life cycle of books'. A unit dedicated to digital printing has been set up in conjunction with Danka Services International, under the name Lightning Print. Ingram provides the experience in working with publishers, Danka the skills in printing and IBM the printing technology. The components were due to come together in 1998 under a pilot scheme. At the outset, Ingram group president Michael Lovett declared: "Lightning Print will be able to leverage the synergies provided by these alliances to meet the demands of today's book marketplace. Print-on-demand promises to revolutionise the publishing industry by extending a book's life cycle in the marketplace indefinitely. Publishers will no longer have to worry about unprofitable print runs and warehousing costs. Ingram is also a major supplier to Amazon.com, the largest Internet bookseller.

"This is even better than the proverbial win-win situation. It's win-win-win for all the key players in the book industry. Publishers win because they sell books that otherwise go out of print; booksellers win because they sell more books and bring in more customers; consumers win because more titles are available; authors win because they continue to receive royalties."

He did not mention printers, but clearly pointed to a way forward for the more astute printers to establish closer links with either publishers or the retail chain. By the end of the century, discussions would have moved on from mere ideas to more concrete negotiations. Only a few years ahead, digital printing will be available at several points in the chain from publisher to consumer.

The concept of an out of print book vanishes with print-on-demand. Provided a digital version of the text exists, it will also be possible to generate a single copy. Even without a digital version of the text, scanning and OCR technology have improved to the point where even a book in poor condition can be retrieved and digitised ready for printing. It will also be possible to bind the digitally printed books in customised bindings to suit a particular individual wanting to build a library in identical bindings.

In the Ingram model, publishers will provide it with the original texts, either as camera ready copy to be scanned into the system, or already in a digital format. When an order is booked, the text for the required title is downloaded to the monochrome Infoprint 4000, or to the colour InfoColor 70 digital press for printing covers. The two parts are tracked using ISBN numbers and put together for delivery to the bookseller placing the order. Production takes three days, with delivery to the end bookseller guaranteed within 15 days.

Under the Lightning system the publisher retains all rights and can print and publish elsewhere. The choice of titles carried is made by the publisher. However the format is standardised: mono text, colour cover, 700pp maximum and 6 x 7" in trade paperback format. There is a single fee for registering the title initially and a nominal fee for holding the title in the database. The end price will be slightly higher to cover the raised production costs.

Ingram is promising at present to continue as a wholesale distributor to booksellers rather than selling direct to consumers. However with its links to Amazon.com, this is likely to be subject to change as circumstances themselves change. Within 10 years, unless other booksellers also adapt, Ingram is likely to be reconsidering this part of its commitment. Before that, the pilot project based in Tennessee is likely to be expanded, first to bring the printing units closer to the company's three distribution centres and, perhaps a stage further, to be closer to the major retail outlets. As Amazon.com opens distribution units in different territories, it is unthinkable that printing will not form part of the expansion, with digital printing alongside the warehouse.

IMPROVEMENTS TO CONVENTIONAL PRINTING

Hand in hand with the move towards digital printing will be improvements to conventional printing, making use of the power of direct-to-plate imaging to cut out an entire production stage and save both time and money. The universal acceptance of pdf, as the format for moving text only pages, made computer-to-plate (CTP) operation not only feasible but essential. All UK book printers will be involved in CTP imaging.

Patrick Bergmans, former president of Belgian company Barco Graphics, which supplied many printers with the systems to cope with CTP, believes that pdf was an essential pre-requisite for book printers. "It's a necessary step towards the industrialisation of the printing industry. Productions costs will have to be reduced, productivity will have to be increased, printing will have to be a more industrial process. The big question now is what will become of pdf. And is the accessing of data going to go beyond the page level? If so, pdf will need to become editable by object. This industry has an increasing need for editing."

That editing will include the ability to change colours to suit the printing process better, for as much as the technology exists to produce books on demand, another future for books lies with higher and higher quality work. There has always been a pleasure in handling books and aesthetic reasons for owning them. As the baby boomer generation reaches middle age, with a satisfactory disposable income, evidence is emerging that well printed books are among their favoured targets for spending. Perhaps books evoke a bygone era when craftsmanship was important. This would certainly account for the popularity of the private presses. These are dedicated crafts people, using printing equipment that Caxton might have designed and would certainly have appreciated. Printing a book by hand is a laborious process, involving type design, hand composition, and one sheet at a time hand printing. The result is a spectacularly beautiful book which has almost certainly sold out its short print run even as the first sheets are being printed. There is enough money around for people to spend £2-300 on a single book, which may well be simply another version of an established classic.

This type of letterpress printing would have little to do with digital technology were it not for the fact that a Scottish engineer/printer has rigged up a Monotype hot metal caster with a computer interface, so that the entire machine can be controlled by an Apple Mac. Digital technology reaches even the oldest of printing processes. The success of the Folio Society, many of whose editions are printed letterpress, indicates that there is a continuing place for traditional printing methods. Indeed it's likely that appreciation of craft technology will grow as a counter to the high tech environment in which people work. Quality will out.

Digital technology will have more impact when printing colour books by conventional means. Despite its investment in digital presses, Butler & Tanner has spent significantly more on standard litho printing machines to print colour books. Other book printing companies have done likewise. The large European companies have invested millions in giant web offset presses, capable of printing tens or hundreds of thousands of pages in an hour. A French company – Jean Maury – will install its third Book-o-matic press early in the new century. Servo motors and computer

control on this machine will make it faster to set up and run than the two similar presses that the company already has. Giant reels of paper are fed in at one end and progress through the huge printing units before the web is slit into different ribbons, passing into the folder and emerging as a folded collated book. Further on-line operations add glue, spine covers if it is to be a limp bound book, or end papers if a case bound title. The book is either delivered from the end of the press complete, or as a block for further finishing. Each book can be hundreds of pages long and can be in two colours. The standard of printing is as high as sheetfed litho, but the costs of production per book are considerably lower than any other method of production currently available.

The reason that such machines are not enormously popular comes from their specialist nature. It is not possible to print magazines or newspapers on them, nor to print many different formats of book. Only the dedicated book printing companies can afford such investment, and then only when backed by a long term commitment from a publisher. For this is to be another feature of the digital age. The investments that are necessary in networks and printing systems are such that they can only be contemplated within the security of long term relationships. This will cause publishers to look hard at the suppliers they use and trim the numbers so that they are working with just a handful of companies. The logical end of this is to do as RR Donnelley has done in the USA, building a new factory just to print Penguin titles for North America. It will also mean that there will be fewer book printers in the new century working with fewer larger publishers.

A NEW GENERATION OF MACHINES

This sort of deal, and the massive investment in conventional, though digitally controlled printing presses, will ensure that litho printing survives alongside digital non-impact printing well into the next century. The two processes will also be combined in a new generation of printing machines. Kodak and Heidelberg, the world's largest printing machine manufacturer, have announced a joint venture to develop an entirely new machine, backed by figures showing that the transition to digital short run printing is unstoppable. Heidelberg will also be working with Creo, a Canadian company whose technical director has some interesting ideas on the future designs of a printing machine. Dan Gelbart has developed what he calls a switchable photopolymer. It is a milky liquid which is coated on to a printing cylinder. A laser is used to write a digital image on the cylinder. Where the laser, tuned to generate heat rather than light energy, strikes the polymer, it becomes hard, leaving an image area represented by the hardened polymer and a non-image area which can be washed off. The image area has ink attracting properties, which the bare cylinder does not. After printing, the polymer can be scrubbed from the cylinder ready for the next application. In this scenario, the printing plate is completely removed from the process, while the benefits of conventional printing, such as speed and quality and low cost per page, are retained.

That press will be ready before 2004, with commercial deliveries beginning shortly after. This technology, or other digital on-press imaging, would be ideal in combination with conventional printing. The immediate application for book printing is in multi-language editions. At present, these are printed on five unit presses, with the fifth unit dedicated to printing the text. The layout of the images is assumed to remain constant whatever the language. As the print run for one edition ends, the press is stopped, the fifth black plate is taken off, a new one loaded and printing restarts. This is faster now that automatic plate changing is available, but using a digitally imaged cylinder instead of a fifth printing plate will speed the process still further and make multi-language printing a much more efficient process.

Colour printing for all types of books, including novels, will increase. Colour will be available at little extra cost and the quality and consistency of the colour, crucial to book printing, will be improved to the point where, once a standard has been set and the colour co-ordinates entered into the press control console, the printing press will not waiver. The entry could come from the printing press operator, or more likely through a digital file that is sent to the press via a fibre optic link. Standards to do this are under development and are being enthusiastically discussed by committees. Leading the chase at present is one called CIP3, for Computer to Prepress, Press and Post press operations. Once a job file has been completed, including the imposition and folds and trims, the file is sent to the press, which automatically adjusts the colour settings to suit, and then to the bindery, where the folding machines and binders will make the adjustments for the new book according to the digital file. The industry is on its way towards an automatic hands off factory.

TRADITION

At the opposite end of the spectrum, a further small, but not insignificant trend in the digital age will be towards hand crafted book printing, where the aesthetic of the book stands in total contrast to the vast amount of digitally produced print and screen-based information displays. At the end of the 19th century and into the early years of the 20th, the Arts and Crafts movement, started by William Morris, stressed the importance of relating industrialised man to what he was making. Book printing was one of the prime examples and one of the fields where Morris himself specialised, starting the Kelmscott Press to pursue these ideals. It was during this period that hot metal typesetting was starting to replace the hand setting skills of compositors of old, and the movement was a reaction to the dehumanising influence of industrialisation.

The Kelmscott Press and others like it, also produced remarkably fine books which are now highly sought after. As the 20th century ends, there remains a flourishing private press movement, run by enthusiasts from workshops often located in rural positions. The demand for the small number of books they produce each year is high, each single printed sheet being treated as a work of art and the machinery – hand operated presses and typesetting, lovingly cared for. The same influences that influenced Morris are again at work. As production moves into the digital age, the beauty of a well printed and bound book will not be ignored.

❿ Conclusion

THE world of publishing in 2010 is going to look very different from that 15 years earlier. Distinctions between publishers and computer software developers, or broadcasters are going to be blurred. Content providers and publishers will be inter-mingled. The technologies to deliver publications of all kinds are going to change, though for most, paper will retain its crucial role. In the case of academic and technical publications, digital will be the dominant medium of delivery. Even where paper retains its place, the production technology that has printed the book, magazine or newspaper will be a digital system or, at the very least, will incorporate elements of digital printing. What is printed is a decision that will be taken by the reader and user of the book or magazine. This might mean placing a digital order through the Internet and having a book printed in direct response to that order. It might also involve readers providing extensive information about their likes and dislikes, so that a publisher may be able to use this information to establish what sorts of magazines are going to sell and exactly who will buy the products.

▲   ▲   ▲

Digital technology by itself is not enough to produce these changes. It will be the development of local networks, wide networks and public networks that provides the catalyst to spark the digital age for publishing. It is sometimes hard to remember that the World Wide Web is only five years old, so pervasive has it become. Estimating what it will develop into in 15 years is perhaps foolish, but it doesn't take a genius to predict that its impact will be substantial. The Internet is going to be as ubiquitous as the telephone, and available in as many varieties, from the large networked digital exchange to the lightweight mobile communications device, perhaps worn on the wrist. For the consumer, the Internet as the public network, will be used to source all kinds of information, to shop, to carry out transactions, to bank and contact friends and family. For business, the private network, an intranet, is going to be used to link internal networks of companies and their clients and suppliers. Process information will be available as never before. Data will slip from one company to another seamlessly.

Once digital networks have been set up, it will be impossible to say where one company ends and the other takes over. Within organisations, the local network will bring work teams together even though they may be in different parts of the building, the city, country or even the world. The world of named offices, paper files, desks and telephone extensions will disappear. Individuals will keep files in secure individual Web sites, accessible across the Internet from any computer with a connection and browser. Working groups will have their own storage area on the Internet, allowing members of that team to take from the pool, work on a task and return it for the next operation. As and when outside suppliers are needed, they too will be drawn into the group. Once the job has finished, the work group can be dissolved and another formed. The workplace of the next century is going to be marked by its extreme fluidity. Rigid hierarchies will disappear.

Perhaps the closest to this concept of the network company is a British software company called Harlequin. It is British only to the extent that it is incorporated under UK law, and has sites scattered around the globe, but no head office building. In the UK there are

Harlequin offices in Cambridge, Manchester and Scotland; in the USA in Seattle, Boston, Texas and California. There are offices in Japan and Australia. All are linked and all have staff collaborating on projects, developing software 24 hours a day. It is, says founder Jo Marks, "a model of the networked company of the future". Software that the company has developed tracks the progress of jobs and ensures that the latest versions are being used. There have been enormous challenges in adopting this way of working but, says Marks, once the initial learning curve has been passed, enormous advantages too.

The Harlequin model for the corporation of the next century will be adopted and altered to suit many companies. The production of newspapers, books and magazines will have to adopt the networked model and many are already edging towards this goal. In newspapers, multitasking and multiple products will lead to the creation of cross product teams, working on paper and electronic products. At any time, the teams might involve writers, freelance help, designers, photographers and subs as well as editors. There will be no need to be in the same physical space. The teams will dissolve and be formed as necessary, with different project leaders if this is required. Book publishers will also move this way, with a greater emphasis on bringing in freelance skills to fill in the gaps where staff were once employed. The networked organisation will be a great boon to the self employed tele-worker. It fits in with a desire to minimise overhead costs at all points in a corporation. Publishers will have to address the issues associated with a shortage of skilled experienced staff.

Teams of editors, designers, authors, publishers and increasingly marketing executives will be put together to guide a project to completion. They will then dissolve and reform with a slightly different mix to handle the next job. In the telephone-led world, this has not been possible because of the dislocation that communication by phone causes. It is a one-to-one system, whereas the Internet provides a many-to-many network, where links between individuals can be as intense or as loose as required.

This sort of development would not be possible without a massive increase in network bandwidth to carry the exponential increase in data traffic. Which solution emerges victorious does not really matter – whether it comes from the current crop of telecommunications companies, or from the power companies passing data as well as electricity along their grids, or whether a network of satellites will provide the unlimited bandwidth. What is certain is that accessing information and passing information across the Internet will not be a problem.

This will enable print-on-demand forms of information delivery, firstly for academic journals and books, and then, increasingly, for time sensitive material. The personalised newspaper is the ultimate and there will be a market for a publication which covers items that are of particular interest to one individual. However the costs and difficulties of producing a publication, the size of even a small tabloid, tailored to one individual, will be prohibitive and the product itself unattractive. Instead, the digital publication that sells will be one where the user selects subjects and perhaps sources (it would be worth reading a favourite columnist for example,) and intelligent agent software, combing the Net will collate this information at a preset time and print it out inside the home. It will then be possible to read this *Daily Me* digest to coincide with the alarm clock.

It will not replace the newspaper however. Events move too fast to be prescribed by the individual. What is of interest one day may be boring the next. And for sheer value for money the newspaper will remain hard to beat. Newspaper publishers will know in far greater detail who their readers are and will be able to target supplements and sections accordingly. Newspaper printing will remain the cheapest type of printing well into the future. The single factory in central London supplying the entire country – the Fleet Street model – will disappear, forced out by a combination of legislation, technology and market pressure. Legislation will limit the use of heavy lorries and so make it uneconomic to shift large tonnages of newsprint by road. Technology improvements will make it easier to print shorter runs and the network will allow the newspaper to be sent digitally to a printing plant closer to the readers. The satellite printing arrangements will provide the potential for local editions, customised with news items for the immediate region.

Competition will push newspaper publishers into providing additional supplements. It is not inconceivable that a newspaper will have a colour supplement for each day of the week. This would not be practical without digital networks controlling editorial, advertising and production systems.

To combat the threat from on-line classified advertising, newspapers must adapt their classified packages accordingly, perhaps by offering electronic and print advertising at a single price, perhaps by offering a group classified sale to produce national coverage for the appropriate ad. Many items sold through classified columns, or jobs advertised in local papers, are of interest to those that are not familiar with technology and unlikely to become so in the next few years. For whatever impact digital technology may have, it is always tempered by the reaction of flesh and blood people. Some may not sign up to the digital age for economic reasons – they cannot afford the initial investment. Others may feel themselves excluded by age or lack of education. Some will exclude themselves deliberately. Electronic information cannot be forced on consumers.

This will safeguard the existence of magazines as well as newspapers. However the digital technology which has made it possible to launch magazines and then withdraw from a non developing market rapidly (IPC's *Eat Soup* lasted just two issues,) will be available to an increasing number of companies. Tomorrow's world will be distinguished, in magazines at least, by fragmentation. Publishers large and small will seek niches and because digital systems have reduced running costs, many more magazines will be launched, only to disappear shortly after. The days when five titles could dominate the world of women's magazines are gone, never to return. The successful consumer magazine in 2010 will be strong in its niche, backed by a large subscription sale and will be supported by an adventurous Web site that continues the magazine's identity between issues.

The business magazine may yield entirely to the Internet, provided a means can be found to retain the revenues from advertising that the printed version obtains. Subscription-only Web sites seem an option, provided the editorial teams can be encouraged to consider a daily, rather than a weekly or monthly deadline. But where display advertising is in decline, thanks partly to mergers reducing the number of suppliers to a market, and partly because spending is directed towards direct mail instead of on-page advertising, Internet publication provides a means of continuing a weaker title, perhaps in combination with a reduced frequency. In the business arena, advertisers may seek to place moving images on a Web site, something that is impossible in a paper product. Alternatively there will be conventional print versions of magazines that start life on the Internet, both for consumer markets and business-to-business readers.

These publishers will be no longer be hide bound into thinking they are publishers of magazines. The phrase 'information providers' will have moved from the lips of consultants and analysts into practice. This applies with even more vigour to academic book and journal publishers, where the printed version is definitely going to take second place to the electronic. In terms of availability, cost reduction and market penetration, the digital media have the potential for far greater impact than print. And as the new century starts, the barriers which have hampered development of electronic products so far – student and tutor resistance and publisher fear – will fade away.

Trade books, novels and illustrated books, will prove resilient to attack by electronic media. However the methods of producing them and delivering them to the reader are going to change radically. People will still want to read books while travelling, for relaxation and on holiday. Reading is essentially a private experience and a printed book reinforces this. However the electronic book will make an appearance and will be adopted by those that positively embrace new technology. In the first instance electronic books will have a specialist appeal to professionals – like lawyers and doctors – who have a wealth of material to read in a given period of time in order to stay up to date with events in their area of work. These professionals will adapt to electronic display for their manuals. Leisure readers however, may prefer to stay with the book, printed on paper and bound between two covers.

John Warnock president and founder of Adobe put it succinctly in a comment to *Wired* magazine: 'There will still be copies of reports you will want to read in your study, still books you'll read in bed at night. There may be a growing appreciation of fine books. After 500 years of tradition and success, paper is certainly not going to go away. But the all consuming, tree consumptive aspect of paper as a transportation medium for information is on the verge of going away, because of the emergence of computers that integrate sound video and print.'

INDEX